SOLID PHASE PEPTIDE SYNTHESIS

The Instrument for Automatic Peptide Synthesis

SOLID PHASE
PEPTIDE SYNTHESIS

JOHN MORROW STEWART
University of Colorado School of Medicine
Denver

AND

JANIS DILLAHA YOUNG
Kaiser Foundation Research Institute
Laboratory of Medical Entomology
San Francisco

FOREWORD BY

R. B. MERRIFIELD
The Rockefeller University
New York

W. H. FREEMAN AND COMPANY
San Francisco

WEBSTER COLLEGE LIBRARY.
470 EAST LOCKWOOD
ST. LOUIS, MISSOURI 63119

Copyright © 1969 by W. H. Freeman and Company

Printed in the United States of America.
Library of Congress Catalog Card Number 69-12604.

FOREWORD

The field of peptide synthesis has successfully maintained its position in the rapidly advancing front of modern science, and during the past decade we have seen major developments in every phase of the subject. Methods of amino acid activation have been greatly extended, and a large array of selectively removable protecting groups has been devised. Problems of racemization and other side-reactions are now much better understood and more readily controlled. The astute application of these new discoveries has led to the synthesis of large numbers of peptides, including many of biological significance. Both the size and the complexity of the peptides that can be synthesized have steadily increased, and we are now close to being able to synthesize true proteins.

Synthetic peptides are important in many areas: to chemists as the ultimate proof of the structure of natural products; to biochemists as models for studying the specificity and mechanism of action of enzymes; to physical chemists as models for the investigation of protein conformation; to pharmacologists as sources of products with modified or selective hormonal activity; to immunologists as tools for defining and understanding immunological specificity—the list could be greatly extended.

Although investigators in these diverse areas are all interested in peptides, they are not all in a position to prepare the particular peptide they require. Methods that will make these compounds more generally available are, therefore, of some importance. Solid phase peptide synthesis was devised and developed with this need in mind. The new approach was expected to accelerate and simplify the task of preparing synthetic peptides. Like many new ideas, this one is very simple in principle. Experimentally, however, there are many details to be considered, and these have changed continually as the method has been developed. With the involvement of more and more laboratories, a continuous flow of modifications of and variations on the original theme has inevitably followed. It is important to have all these experimental details gathered together in one place and to have them critically evaluated.

The authors of this volume have done a valuable service for those who would learn the new method and who wish to prepare their own peptides in this way. It is an authoritative account by two who have contributed to the methodology themselves and who have had the necessary experience to understand the techniques. Furthermore, they appreciate the inherent limitations as well as the advantages of the method, and are fully aware of the great importance of thoroughly characterizing the products of synthesis and of evaluating their purity.

This volume is intended to be a laboratory manual that will provide all the experimental detail required by even a relative novice in the field. The newcomer will also appreciate the theory and discussion which accompany the experimental material.

The ready preparation of peptides is a practical reality and the chemical synthesis of proteins is clearly a feasible goal. The experimental approach described in this book is expected to play an important role in attaining that goal.

May 1968   *R. B. Merrifield*

PREFACE

Solid phase peptide synthesis was developed by R. B. Merrifield in order to simplify and accelerate peptide synthesis in a way that would make the synthesis of long peptides practical and be amenable to further acceleration by automation. That both these goals have been realized in the few years since the original announcement of the technique speaks well for the soundness of the concept. Descriptions of the synthesis by this method of a wide variety of peptides of chain lengths up to fifty-five amino acid residues have appeared in the literature. An instrument for the automatic synthesis of peptides by this method has been described and is under commercial development.

The wide interest engendered by these disclosures has come not only from established peptide chemists, who have realized that much of the drudgery of their work could be eliminated, but also from other scientists, who have perceived that materials for a wide range of physical, chemical, and biological studies would now be readily accessible.

The space limitations imposed by scientific journals have minimized the experimental detail in the published reports of the solid phase method, and many persons who have tried to use or would like to use the method have expressed a desire for a fuller description of the laboratory procedures used. It is in response to such requests that this book is offered. In addition, we have learned from our own experience that one of the most time-consuming and important aspects of executing a laboratory procedure is locating the proper apparatus and chemicals. We have therefore compiled, in Appendixes A, B, and C, a rather complete list of the apparatus, glassware, and chemicals that are necessary for solid phase peptide synthesis, and of the manufacturers and dealers who can supply these materials.

The data in this book represent the state of the art of solid phase synthesis at the time of writing, to our best knowledge. In a field as new as this one, progress is rapid, and it is to be expected that many changes and improvements will appear within a few years. We invite workers in the field to send us information about improvements in technique and new chemical procedures, and a record of peptides synthesized, so that future up-to-date editions may be facilitated.

Finally, the information contained in this manual is a record of experience with certain specific peptides. As one gains more knowledge of the chemistry of different peptides, it becomes apparent that different types of peptides have their own unique physical and chemical characteristics. These different characteristics may mean that the standard or special conditions of synthesis developed for one group of peptides may not apply to the synthesis of other peptides. We recommend that persons beginning to use the method first establish some competence by repeating a solid phase synthesis described in the literature. Then, if difficulty is encountered with some new peptide, the cause of the trouble can be more readily ascertained, and suitable modifications can be applied to overcome the obstacle.

We are deeply indebted to Bruce Merrifield, for, in addition to his original development of the solid phase method, he has unstintingly given us many hours of advice and suggestions, and has given permission to use much unpublished information. We also deeply appreciate his reading and criticism of the entire manuscript. Our thanks also go to many other friends for their permission to include important unpublished data. Special thanks go to Art Robinson, of the University of California, San Diego, to Bob Samuels, of the Spinco Division, Beckman Instruments, Palo Alto, California, and to Leslie Holybee, of the Department of Biochemistry, Stanford University Medical School, for the sections they contributed. We thank Arnold Marglin for many suggestions, particularly on the sodium reduction, and for a critical reading of the entire manuscript.

John M. Stewart
Janis D. Young

May 1968

CONTENTS

FIGURES

Frontispiece: The automatic instrument for SPPS.

SOLID PHASE PEPTIDE SYNTHESIS

ABBREVIATIONS

The abbreviations used throughout this work are essentially those recommended by the IUPAC-IUB Commission on Biochemical Nomenclature, as published in *J. Biol. Chem.* **241**, 2491 (1966), and **242**, 555 (1967), also in *Biochem.* **5**, 2485 (1966), and **6**, 362 (1967).

APM	aminopeptidase M
Aoc	*t*-amyloxycarbonyl
Boc	*t*-butyloxycarbonyl
Bu	butyl
Bzl	benzyl
CCD	countercurrent distribution
DCC	dicyclohexylcarbodiimide
DMF	dimethylformamide
Dnp	2,4-dinitrophenyl
Et	ethyl
EtOAc	ethyl acetate
EtOH	ethanol (absolute)
FDNB	1-fluoro-2,4-dinitrobenzene
HOAc	acetic acid (glacial)
Me	methyl
Nps	*o*-nitrophenylsulfenyl
Pr	propyl
SPPS	solid phase peptide synthesis
TFA	trifluoroacetic acid, anhydrous
TLC	thin-layer chromatography
Tos	*p*-toluenesulfonyl
Z	carbobenzoxy (benzyloxycarbonyl)
Ztf	1-carbobenzoxamido-2,2,2-trifluoroethyl

1

THE CHEMISTRY
OF SOLID PHASE
PEPTIDE SYNTHESIS

The basic principles of solid phase peptide synthesis and a summary of the chemistry now used for such synthesis are given in this chapter. More consideration of the problems that were encountered in developing the current method and of how they were solved, as well as detailed instructions on how to use the method, will be given in the succeeding chapters. We have assumed that the reader will have a working knowledge of classical peptide synthesis, excellent coverage of which is already available (13, 31, 113); we will therefore not repeat it here, except insofar as it directly concerns solid phase synthesis.

The fundamental premise of solid phase peptide synthesis is that amino acids can be assembled into a peptide of any desired sequence while one end of the chain is anchored to an insoluble support. After the desired sequence of amino acids has been linked together on the support, a reagent can be applied to cleave the chain from the support and liberate the finished peptide into solution. All the reactions involved in the synthesis can be brought to 100 per cent completion, so that a homogeneous product can be obtained. The great virtue of using a solid support is that all the laborious purification at intermediate steps in the synthesis is eliminated, and simple washing and filtration of the solid is substituted. By using a suitably designed vessel,

all the synthesis can be carried out in that vessel without any transferring of material from one container to another. Mechanical loss of material in the transfer operations is thus eliminated.

This basic idea is illustrated in Figure 1. The solid support is a synthetic polymer that bears reactive groups (X). These groups are made to react with the carboxyl group of an amino acid in such a way that the amino acid is bound covalently to the polymer. During this step, the amine group of the amino acid must be covered with a protecting group (Y) so that the amine will not react with the polymer. The protecting group must be such that it can be selectively removed without damage to the bond holding the amino acid to the support. After removal of this protecting group, a second N-protected amino acid can be caused to acylate the exposed amine group of the first amino acid, thus forming the first peptide bond. By repeating these two deprotection and coupling steps, using each time the proper N-protected amino acid, the peptide of desired sequence is assembled on the polymer support. At the end of the synthesis, a different reagent is applied to cleave specifically the bond joining the first amino acid to the polymer, and the free peptide is liberated into solution.

The chemistry involved in the most com-

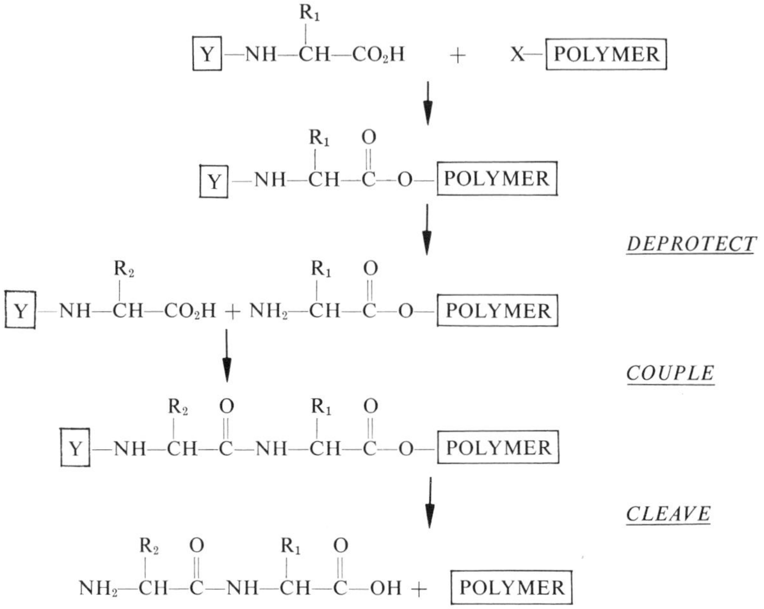

FIGURE 1.
The Basic Plan of Solid Phase Peptide Synthesis.

monly used system of solid phase synthesis (72) is shown in Figure 2. The solid support is a synthetic resin, a copolymer of styrene and divinylbenzene, which bears reactive chloromethyl groups. This chloromethyl resin reacts with the salt of a *t*-butyloxycarbonyl amino acid to form an ester bond between the amino acid and the resin. The *t*-butyloxycarbonyl protecting group is selectively removed by treatment of the protected aminoacyl resin with anhydrous hydrogen chloride in an organic solvent, usually either dioxane or acetic acid. The aminoacyl resin hydrochloride which results from this treatment is then treated with a solution of triethyl amine to neutralize the hydrochloride and liberate the free amine group in a condition ready for coupling with the next amino acid. The *t*-butyloxycarbonyl derivative of the next amino acid desired in the peptide chain is then added, along with a coupling agent, usually dicyclohexylcarbodiimide. (Other coupling agents or amino acid active esters can be used at this step to introduce the new amino acid.) The protected dipeptide-resin which results from this coupling step can be then treated as many times as desired with this sequence of three steps—deprotection, neutralization, and coupling of the new amino acid—until the desired peptide is linked together on the resin. Throughout all these operations, reagents and reaction conditions are chosen so that all reactions go to 100 per cent completion. The only purification used at any step is the washing of the resin and its attached peptide with appropriate solvents, which can be handled simply, rapidly, and effectively. The finished peptide-resin is then suspended in anhydrous trifluoroacetic acid, and a slow stream of hydrogen bromide is bubbled through the suspension. This reagent removes the *t*-butyloxycarbonyl protecting group by an elimination reaction, and cleaves the finished peptide from the resin by a nucleophilic displacement reaction. Certain other protecting groups used for amino acid side-chain functions are simultaneously removed from the peptide, but peptide bonds are not harmed. Any side-chain protecting groups that are stable to the treatment can then be removed by an appropriate reagent, and the synthetic peptide then purified by a suitable technique.

Solid phase synthesis can best be considered a special case of stepwise synthesis of peptides from the C-terminus (the carboxyl end of a peptide). The linkage of the C-terminal amino acid to the resin is in effect a substituted benzyl ester, and the chemistry of solid phase synthesis is essentially that used in the stepwise synthesis of a peptide benzyl ester in solution, except that it has not as yet been possible to cleave peptides from the resin by hydrogenolysis. Another major difference in solid phase synthesis is that all the reactions must go to 100 per cent com-

pletion if a homogeneous product is to be obtained, since there is no purification of intermediates during the synthesis. In practice, this difference means that a stronger reagent and a longer reaction time than would normally be needed for complete removal must be used to remove the amine protecting groups, and that several moles of each new activated amino acid must be used to insure complete introduction of that amino acid residue. There will thus be some waste of amino acids, especially when the diimide coupling method is used, for with that

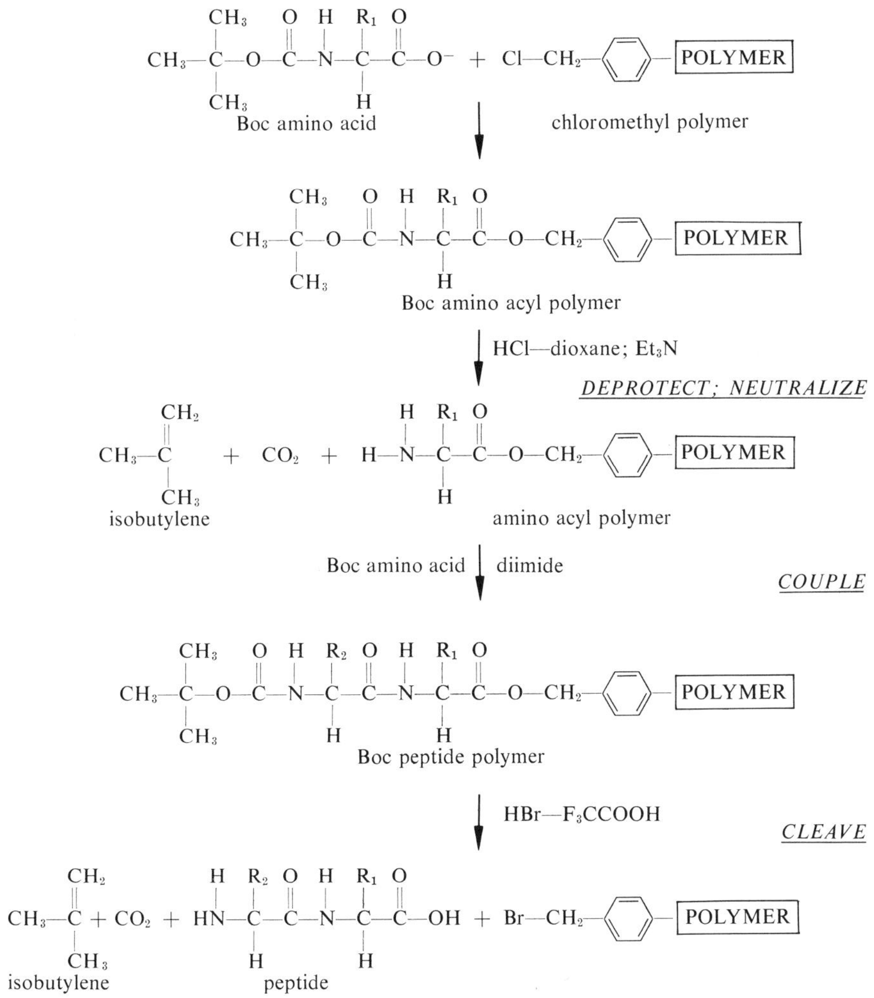

FIGURE 2.
Chemical Reactions Used in Solid Phase Peptide Synthesis.

method the excess reagent cannot be recovered (the reactive intermediate rearranges to the stable acyl urea and is lost as a by-product). Generally, however, the greatly increased speed of operation possible with solid phase synthesis and the over-all yields, which are usually excellent, more than offset this disadvantage. Theoretically, amino acid derivatives could be recovered when active esters are used for coupling.

One great advantage of the stepwise method of peptide synthesis from the carboxyl end, which is used in the Merrifield system of solid phase synthesis, is the general freedom from racemization. In this technique, only the carboxyl groups of amino-protected single amino acids are activated for coupling, never the carboxyl groups of peptides. This approach has been found to assure freedom from racemization, both in classical peptide synthesis in solution and in the Merrifield method, when the carbobenzoxy or t-butyloxycarbonyl protecting groups are used. Limited experience thus far indicates that the o-nitrophenylsulfenyl protecting group can also be used. This would seem to be a significant advantage of the Merrifield method over that proposed by Letsinger (54), in which the peptide is assembled from the amino end and in which each coupling step after the first involves activation of a peptide carboxyl, with the attendant danger of racemization.

The stepwise approach to synthesis does have some limitations, particularly with a program to synthesize structural variants of a single type of molecule. In block synthesis, various small fragments can be combined in many ways, to furnish a wide variety of different analogs. Stepwise synthesis from the carboxyl end is especially convenient for preparing structural variants near the amino end of the peptide, as in the application of the Merrifield method to the synthesis of bradykinin analogs (127, 128, 132), where a large batch of peptide-resin containing the C-terminal part of the molecule has been prepared, and aliquots of this resin used for making the structural variants of the N-terminal part. The solid phase method is not as versatile for preparing variants of the C-terminal part of the molecule, since the synthesis must be essentially started anew for each variant.

Thus far the block method of peptide synthesis, in which short peptides are coupled together to form long ones, has not been generally applied to solid phase synthesis, although in principle it should be possible to couple short peptides as well as single amino acids to the resin. There has been one report of the coupling of a dipeptide in solid phase (141), and a report of the successful coupling of ε-aminocaproic acid tetramers (102). This approach might be particularly useful for the synthesis of peptides with repeating sequences, such as are found in the collagen field. If a practical limit to the length of peptides that can be satisfactorily assembled by the solid phase method is found in the future, it might still be possible to synthesize very long chains by preparing shorter pieces by the solid phase method and then combining them in solution; one laboratory is already using this approach (93), but in using it, the protecting groups used for side-chain functional groups must be chosen with exceptional care. One possibility might be to use t-butyl esters for glutamic and aspartic protection and o-nitrophenylsulfenyl for the α-amino groups of amino acids. The nitrophenylsulfenyl groups could be removed by the thioamide method, the peptide could be cleaved from the resin by hydrazinolysis, and the azide method could then be used for joining the component peptides together. One special problem of this approach would be racemization, which often occurs when peptides are activated for coupling. The methods of synthesis and the points for the breaks in the chain would have to be chosen with special care to circumvent this difficulty.

The problems of strategy in the Merrifield method concern the establishment and cleavage of the bond linking the peptide to the resin support, the protection and deprotection of α-amino groups and side-chain functional groups, and the choice of coupling methods, all of which are intimately interconnected. The C-terminal amino acid must be attached to the resin support by a bond which will be stable to all the reagents used during the synthetic assembly of the desired amino acid sequence on the resin, yet which can be selectively cleaved at the end of the synthesis in such a way that no peptide bond or amino acid residue will be harmed. For the side-chain functions of trifunctional amino acids, protecting groups which are stable to the conditions of synthesis, but can be removed selectively from the finished peptide, must be used.

The techniques currently in use for the Merrifield method have enabled investigators to synthesize a wide range of peptides containing all the natural amino acids. The largest peptides synthesized by this method so far are insulin (62), with its two chains of 21 and 30 amino acid residues, and ferredoxin (6), with 55 residues. Solid phase syntheses have been carried out on a scale ranging all the way from 10 mg of resin [two micromoles of peptide (121)] to 40 g of decapeptide-resin in one run (56). The speed of solid phase synthesis, which allows manual synthesis of peptide chains at the rate of two or three residues per day, has been increased to six amino acids per day by the use of an automatic instrument (81, 82). Further developments of this method in the future will doubtless allow even more dramatic progress in peptide synthesis.

Peptides have been prepared by the solid phase method for a variety of purposes. Many naturally occurring peptides have been synthesized (see Appendix F, p. 86), as well as modifications of them for study of structure-activity correlations (47, 95, 128, 132, 135, 139). Peptides have been prepared for studies of immunogenesis (9, 100) and physical-chemical properties (134). One disputed point in the amino acid sequence of a protein was settled by solid phase synthesis of both possible partial sequences and comparison with natural material (144). Many other applications of solid phase synthesis will doubtless appear.

Solid phase synthesis may also prove to be particularly useful in the synthesis of cyclic peptides, since the desired intramolecular reaction can be favored over the undesirable polymerization. In one example of this approach, the disulfide bridge of oxytocin was formed on the resin, and the peptide was then cleaved by ammonolysis (40). The resin used was a phenol-formaldehyde polymer. Katchalski and his co-workers have also used polymeric active esters for the synthesis of cyclic peptides (27).

CHEMICAL ASPECTS OF THE RESIN SUPPORT

A suitable insoluble support and a satisfactory means of attaching the first amino acid to it are of the greatest importance for successful solid phase synthesis of peptides. The solid support must have a physical size and shape that will permit ready manipulation and rapid filtration from liquids. It must be fully inert to all the reagents used during the synthesis of peptides, yet it must be modifiable in some way that will allow ready attachment of an amino acid to it by a covalent bond. The solid support chosen by Merrifield after a long search was composed of fine beads (20–70 microns in diameter) of a synthetic resin prepared by copolymerization of styrene with 2 per cent divinylbenzene. This polymer is composed of long alkyl chains bearing a phenyl ring on every second carbon. These chains are crosslinked at approximately every fiftieth carbon by p-diethylphenyl residues derived from the divinylbenzene. This crosslinking causes the polymer to be completely insoluble in all ordinary solvents. The low degree of crosslinking gives a resin that swells extensively in certain organic solvents, but is yet chemically inert during peptide synthesis. The swelling in solvents is very important, since many of the peptide chains on the resin are attached within the pores and interstices of the beads, and swelling is necessary for satisfactory penetration of solvents and reagents to these growing points. The resin generally used, a commercial product prepared

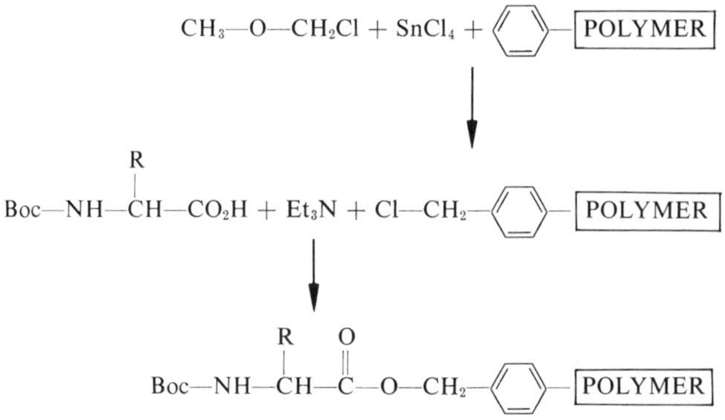

$$CH_3—O—CH_2Cl + SnCl_4 + \langle \bigcirc \rangle—\boxed{POLYMER}$$

$$\downarrow$$

$$\overset{\displaystyle R}{\underset{\displaystyle |}{Boc—NH—CH—CO_2H}} + Et_3N + Cl—CH_2—\langle \bigcirc \rangle—\boxed{POLYMER}$$

$$\downarrow$$

$$\overset{\displaystyle R \quad\; O}{\underset{\displaystyle | \qquad ||}{Boc—NH—CH—C—O—CH_2—\langle \bigcirc \rangle—\boxed{POLYMER}}}$$

FIGURE 3.
Attachment of *t*-Butyloxycarbonyl Amino Acids to the Resin.

by the Dow Chemical Company as a starting material for ion-exchange resin, swells extensively in chloroform, dichloromethane, dioxane, dimethylformamide, and benzene, but swells much less in alcohols, ethyl acetate, and acetic acid. It has been used for most of the solid phase syntheses reported, although one synthesis was carried out with better results using a 1 per cent crosslinked resin (75). The 2 per cent resin is commercially available (see Appendix C).

The amino acid that will become the C-terminal residue of the synthetic peptide is attached to the resin by its carboxyl group, the amine group being protected meanwhile. This protected amino acid is attached by an ester bond—a covalent bond—not by ion exchange, as some have erroneously thought (see Figure 3). In order to effect this esterification of the amino acid to the resin, the polymer must first be made reactive. Suitable procedures for performing such activation are available from polymer chemistry. The benzene rings in a polystyrene-divinylbenzene resin can be conveniently chloromethylated in a Friedel-Crafts reaction with chloromethyl methyl ether and stannic chloride. The halogen thus introduced is in a reactive benzyl chloride type of linkage, and is subject to facile nucleophilic displacement reactions. Carboxylate anions can effect such a displacement of highly activated halogens, giving rise to esters in a reaction similar to one used by

organic chemists to prepare derivatives from acids—namely, the reaction of acid salts with phenacyl halides.

The degree of chloromethylation of the resin can be controlled by adjusting the conditions of the chloromethylation reaction, and can be measured by elemental analysis of the resin for chlorine or, more conveniently, by displacement of the chlorine by a tertiary amine, followed by Volhard determination of the liberated chloride. Most of the work so far has been done with chloromethyl resins containing one to two millimoles of chlorine per gram of resin. Merrifield has suggested that resins which are more highly chloromethylated might cause difficulty, since peptide chains might start in very small pores of the resin beads, pores that are too small to allow the chains to grow to their desired length. The recommended degree of chloromethylation does not appear to lead to this problem.

It is evident that the chloromethyl groups on the resin are not of uniform reactivity. It is virtually impossible to displace all of them with amino acid residues. Even when only a small fraction of the chlorines are replaced by amino acids, these amino acids are not equally reactive, since some of them never enter into the chain-forming reactions and can be recovered upon cleavage of the peptide from the resin. Although these excesses of potentially reactive groups have been a cause for concern, there has been no evidence that they interfere with satisfactory peptide synthesis.

Attachment of the first amino acid to the resin

Carbobenzoxy or *t*-butyloxycarbonyl amino acids can be satisfactorily esterified to the chloromethylated polystyrene-divinylbenzene resin in refluxing absolute ethanol. However, ethyl acetate can also be used as the solvent, and apparently must be used in order to esterify these amino acid derivatives to the nitrated resin which is sometimes used (see pp. 13, 27). The protected amino acid is introduced into the reaction mixture as a salt. For this purpose a base must be chosen which will yield a salt soluble in the organic solvent used for the esterification. Although triethyl amine salts have given satisfactory yields of esterified protected amino acids, the use of a tertiary amine does cause one side reaction which must be considered. The chloromethyl resin will react with triethyl amine to form quaternary triethylammonium groups on the resin (Figure 4). These groups are strong base ion exchangers, and although most of them probably remain as chloride salts throughout the synthesis, there is some evidence that small amounts of protected amino acids may be held to these groups on the resin. The evidence is that the crude product obtained at the close of a synthesis usually contains, in addition to the desired peptide, a small amount of the amino acid that was added last. If a deprotection step with hydrogen chloride is added after the last coupling, this free amino acid is usually not found in the crude product.

The free amino acids are thus most likely held by ion exchange to the resin. Since they are removed by the deprotection step, there is no danger that they would contaminate succeeding coupling steps of the synthesis. It is also possible that free amino acid could arise after diimide syntheses from some of the acyl urea by-product that has not been completely washed out of the resin.

In an attempt to minimize the formation of quarternary groups, Merrifield introduced the practice of using slightly less than one equivalent of triethyl amine in the esterification reaction. The presence of quaternary groups also means that elemental analysis for nitrogen cannot be used to measure the amount of the first amino acid on the resin. Indeed, for this purpose, as well as for general analytical work in all peptide synthesis, suitable procedures or instrumentation for quantitative amino acid analysis are absolutely essential. Elemental analysis has proved to be totally inadequate for determination of the purity of peptides, and many experienced peptide chemists no longer waste their time and facilities in obtaining such analyses. The only satisfactory method for determining the amount of amino acid on the resin is acid hydrolysis followed by quantitative amino acid analysis. The hydrolysis must be carried out in a solvent which swells and wets the resin. A mixture of equal parts of dioxane and concentrated hydrochloric acid is generally used for this purpose.

Usually relatively few of the chlorine molecules on the resin are replaced by amino acid residues in the esterification step. Removal of the remaining chlorine has been attempted (11), but experience has shown that the chlorine apparently does not interfere with any of the

$$Et_3N + Cl—CH_2—\boxed{POLYMER} \longrightarrow Et_3N^+—CH_2—\boxed{POLYMER}$$
$$Cl^-$$

FIGURE 4.
Formation of Ion-Exchange Groups on the Resin.

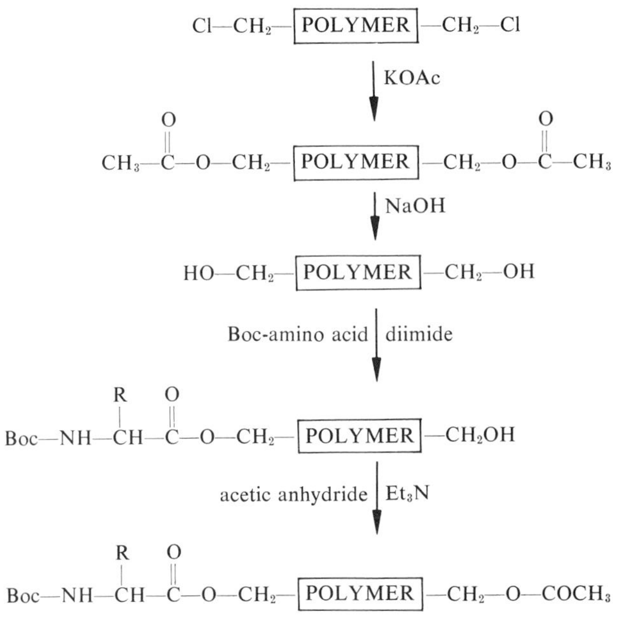

$$Cl-CH_2-\boxed{POLYMER}-CH_2-Cl$$

$$\downarrow KOAc$$

$$CH_3-\overset{\overset{\displaystyle O}{\|}}{C}-O-CH_2-\boxed{POLYMER}-CH_2-O-\overset{\overset{\displaystyle O}{\|}}{C}-CH_3$$

$$\downarrow NaOH$$

$$HO-CH_2-\boxed{POLYMER}-CH_2-OH$$

$$\text{Boc-amino acid} \mid \text{diimide}$$

$$Boc-NH-\overset{\overset{\displaystyle R}{|}}{CH}-\overset{\overset{\displaystyle O}{\|}}{C}-O-CH_2-\boxed{POLYMER}-CH_2OH$$

$$\text{acetic anhydride} \mid Et_3N$$

$$Boc-NH-\overset{\overset{\displaystyle R}{|}}{CH}-\overset{\overset{\displaystyle O}{\|}}{C}-O-CH_2-\boxed{POLYMER}-CH_2-O-COCH_3$$

FIGURE 5.
Formation and Use of Hydroxymethyl Resin.

subsequent synthetic steps and can be ignored for all practical purposes. Most of the solid phase syntheses done so far have used resins bearing from 0.1 to 0.5 millimoles of amino acid per gram of substituted resin, although more highly esterified resins have been used (56). This degree of esterification has generally been obtainable by a 24-hour reaction of the chloromethyl resin with the triethylammonium salt of t-butyloxycarbonyl amino acids in refluxing ethanol. For t-butyloxycarbonyl nitroarginine, a reaction time of 60 to 70 hours is needed, and in the one example of the esterification of t-butyloxycarbonyl S-benzyl cysteine (85), a reaction time of 48 hours was used. At these levels of substitution, peptide chain formation has proceeded satisfactorily, and, except for one peptide (75), there has been no evidence that steric hindrance might interfere with the synthesis of peptides of at least 55 amino acid residues (6).

Dorman and Love (22) converted chloro-methyl resin to a sulfonium salt by reaction with dimethyl sulfide. When the salt of a t-butyloxycarbonyl amino acid with this sulfonium resin was heated briefly, the amino acid was quantitatively esterified to the resin. Although synthesis of peptides from such resins has not yet been reported, the high yield reported makes this esterification procedure attractive, especially for use with very expensive (e.g., radioactive) amino acids.

As was to be expected, amino acids which contain easily alkylatable functional groups cause difficulty in the esterification reaction. Such amino acids are histidine, cysteine, and methionine. When the esterification of t-butyloxycarbonyl-im-benzylhistidine to the chloromethyl resin was attempted, the resin gained the expected amount of weight, but little benzylhistidine could be recovered by acid hydrolysis. Apparently the chloromethyl resin had alkylated the imidazole ring of the histidine to yield a stable histidine-resin derivative (131). A successful alternative was found in the use of a hydroxymethyl resin, to which the histidine derivative was esterified by the action of dicyclohexylcarbodiimide (Figure 5). For synthesis of the hydroxymethyl resin, the chloromethyl resin was first, by reaction with potassium acetate, converted to an acetoxymethyl resin. The latter material was then saponified with alkali. Although the diimide-mediated esterification of t-butyloxycarbonyl-im-benzylhistidine to the hydroxymethyl resin yielded a highly substituted product (0.85 millimoles of amino acid per gram of resin), some hydroxyl groups of the resin remained unacylated. Since the remainder of the synthesis was also to be done by diimide condensations, these resin hydroxyl groups had to be covered if a homogeneous peptide was to be produced. The t-butyloxycarbonyl-im-benzylhistidine-resin was therefore acetylated with acetic anhydride and triethyl amine in dimethylformamide. The remainder of the synthesis was then carried out in the usual way (131).

Very recently, it has been found that α-t-butyloxycarbonyl-im-dinitrophenyl histidine can be esterified in the normal way to the chloromethyl resin (128). Evidently the dinitrophenyl residue lowers the basicity of the imidazole ring sufficiently to protect it from alkylation by the chloromethyl groups on the resin.

A hydroxymethyl resin has also been prepared by Bodanszky and Sheehan (15), who then used carbonyldiimidazole as a coupling agent for the esterification of the first protected amino acid, and nitrophenyl esters for the remainder of the coupling reactions in the synthesis of a peptide. Since amino acid nitrophenyl esters normally do not esterify alcohols, they did not find it necessary to acetylate or otherwise cover the unreacted hydroxyl groups on the resin. They proposed hydroxymethyl resins for general use because of the mild conditions under which amino acids can be attached to them. There is not yet sufficient evidence to establish the superiority of this approach for general work and to justify the additional work involved. One other brief report of the use of a hydroxymethyl resin has appeared (111), in which an unspecified amino acid was esterified to the hydroxymethyl resin by dimethylformamide di-t-amyl acetal.

Of the sulfur-containing amino acids, surprisingly, t-butyloxycarbonyl S-benzyl cysteine was esterified to the chloromethyl resin without difficulty (85). Perhaps less surprisingly, t-butyloxycarbonyl methionine did not esterify satisfactorily to the chloromethyl resin. Preliminary data indicate that this derivative can be esterified to the hydroxymethyl resin by using the carbonyldiimidazole procedure (see p. 33), but not by using dicyclohexylcarbodiimide (60).

Cleavage of the finished peptide from the resin

The most commonly used reaction for removing finished peptides from the resin support has been nucleophilic displacement of the peptide by hydrogen bromide in an anhydrous trifluoroacetic acid medium (Figure 6). This treatment also removes certain of the protecting groups—N-carbobenzoxy, N-t-butyloxycarbonyl, N-o-nitrophenylsulfenyl, and O-benzyl (ethers of serine, threonine, and tyrosine, as well as esters of aspartic and glutamic acids)—that are used in the synthesis. Commonly used groups that remain intact after this treatment are S-benzyl (cysteine), imidazole N-benzyl (histidine), N-nitro (arginine), N-toluenesulfonyl (arginine) and O-p-nitrobenzyl (aspartic and glutamic acids); these are usually removed by further treatment of the peptide with sodium in liquid ammonia or by catalytic hydrogenolysis. When tyrosine-containing peptides are cleaved, the hydrogen bromide should first be scrubbed by bubbling through a tube containing resorcinol or anisole in trifluoroacetic acid to remove any bromine present, otherwise bromotyrosine may be found in the peptide. During the cleavage of peptides containing cysteine, methionine, or tyrosine in addition to O-benzyl or N-carbobenzoxy groups, a scavenger, such as ethyl methyl sulfide (32), triethyl phosphite (42),

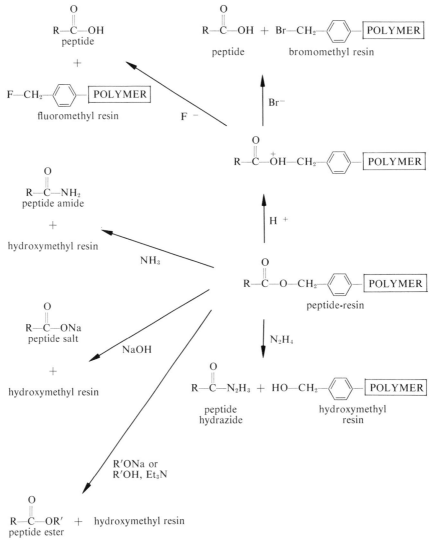

FIGURE 6.
Cleavage of Peptides from the Resin.

methionine (62), or anisole, must be present to prevent damage to these residues by benzylation. Cleavage by hydrogen bromide in trifluoroacetic acid should not be used with peptides containing tryptophan, since complete recovery of the tryptophan in this procedure has not as yet been possible (64). Either anhydrous hydrogen fluoride or one of the base-catalyzed methods (transesterification, ammonolysis, hydrazinolysis, or saponification) should be used, since they do not damage tryptophan.

Since hydrogen bromide is not very soluble in trifluoroacetic acid, the cleavage is performed by suspending the peptide-resin in the solvent and bubbling a slow stream of anhydrous hydrogen bromide through the suspension for 60 to 90 minutes. Recovery of peptides with this method of cleavage has been excellent. For example, in the synthesis of bradykinin analogs, as much as 85 per cent of the first amino acid attached to the resin has been recovered in the purified peptide (128). Yields of other types of peptides have ranged from 85 per cent down to about 50 per cent. Yields will be lower, of course, if there is an incomplete reaction at any step. The yield of peptide from the cleavage cannot be estimated from the dry weight of the crude product, because this reagent also removes a significant amount of nonpeptide material, which is usually water-insoluble, from the resin. This nonpeptide material has routinely been ignored, since it is effectively removed by all purification methods. Although its nature has not been investigated, it may be a degradation product of the resin itself. It has been shown that this cleavage procedure does not cause aspartic acid residues in angiotensin to shift from α-linkage to β-linkage (65), although in one peptide containing an aspartyl-seryl linkage some β-aspartyl peptide was produced via a cyclic intermediate (75). Some workers have questioned the wisdom of and the need for long cleavage times. Almost all the peptide which can ultimately be removed from the resin is cleaved in the first few minutes (30, 65; see p. 35), and with angiotensin (65) cleavage for more than five minutes yielded material which resisted the action of leucine-aminopeptidase, although it did not migrate electrophoretically like the β-aspartyl peptide. A solution of hydrogen bromide in acetic acid could probably be used for cleavage of peptides from the resin (71), but with this reagent threonine and serine residues are acetylated on their hydroxyl groups (32).

Anhydrous liquid hydrogen fluoride (b.p. 19°) has been recently applied to cleavage of peptide-resins, as well as to deprotection of peptides in solution. Sakakibara has shown that suitable protecting groups, removable by hydrogen fluoride, are available for nearly all side-chain functions (105), and has demonstrated the usefulness of hydrogen fluoride for syntheses of oxytocin (104) and vasopressin (106). Robinson (52) applied this reagent to solid phase synthesis, and recent experience in several laboratories has shown it to have great potential for solid phase. Peptides are effectively cleaved from the resin by a treatment of 30 to 45 minutes with hydrogen fluoride at 0°. This

treatment also removes carbobenzoxy, t-butyloxycarbonyl, O-benzyl, O-t-butyl and N-nitro (arginine) protecting groups, but p-nitrobenzyl esters are not cleaved. Removal of S-benzyl from cysteine in 30 minutes requires a temperature of 20°, but S-p-methoxybenzyl is removed readily at 0°. Since im-benzyl histidine is not deprotected by this reagent, histidine is the sole amino acid residue which has not been satisfactorily deprotected in solid phase synthesis by hydrogen fluoride. However, the new 1-carbobenzoxamido-2,2,2-trifluoroethyl protecting group of Weygand (141) should be suitable. Another potentially useful protecting group for the imidazole ring is the 2,4-dinitrophenyl residue. This group can be cleaved from histidine by treatment with thiols at pH 8 (119), it appears to be stable to all the synthetic procedures, and preliminary synthetic experiments with it are promising (57). If these new groups prove to be satisfactory for histidine protection, liquid hydrogen fluoride will probably evolve as the reagent of choice for cleavage and deprotection of peptides. With this reagent, as with hydrogen bromide in trifluoroacetic acid, suitable scavengers must be present to protect sensitive amino acid residues; Sakakibara has found anisole to be quite effective for this purpose (106). Limited experience so far indicates that the yields of peptides obtained from peptide-resins by hydrogen fluoride cleavage may be somewhat lower than those obtained with hydrogen bromide in trifluoroacetic acid. However, the greater versatility of hydrogen fluoride for removing side-chain protecting groups may well offset this disadvantage. In addition, hydrogen fluoride removes less nonpeptide material from the resin than is usually obtained with hydrogen bromide in trifluoroacetic acid. Tryptophan appears to be stable to anhydrous hydrogen fluoride (64). It should be borne in mind that anhydrous hydrogen fluoride on long contact has promoted N–O shifts in serine and threonine peptides (108), and has cleaved methionyl peptides (53). However, in the short times needed to cleave peptides from the resin and to remove protecting groups, these reactions should not be a serious problem. Although anhydrous hydrogen fluoride is highly toxic and corrosive, suitable equipment is available (see pp. 41–44) for making its transfer and use safe.

Saponification, although not now generally used to remove peptides from the resin in solid phase synthesis, was the first cleavage method used by Merrifield (71), and may sometimes be desirable. Merrifield used two successive one-hour treatments of the peptide-resin at 25° with 0.2 N sodium hydroxide in 90 per cent ethanol. Recovery of a tetrapeptide by this procedure was about 50 per cent. Higher yields might be obtained by the use of a solvent, such as dioxane, which promotes better swelling of the resin. One brief account has reported the cleavage of a peptide, His-Phe-Arg-Try-Gly, from the resin (presumably nonnitrated) by sodium ethoxide in ethanol, with a yield of 60 per cent (55).

Very recently a successful method has been developed for removing peptides from the resin by transesterification with an alcohol in the presence of triethyl amine (56), or in the presence of a strong anion-exchange resin (B. Halpern, personal communication). By either method, peptide methyl esters have been easily prepared and in good yield. No racemization was found, as determined by gas-liquid chromatography, with either method of transesterification using dipeptide-resins (B. Halpern). Higher alcohols have also been used. It must be kept in mind that in transesterification, the usual protecting esters on the ω-carboxyls of aspartic and glutamic acids are also transesterified, and steps such as those used with ammonolysis must be taken to circumvent their conversion. Although it has not yet been reported, the use of a nitro resin should facilitate transesterification.

Ammonolysis of peptide-resins provides a way to synthesize peptide amides by the solid phase method. Bodanszky (14) reported the successful synthesis of the C-terminal tripeptide amide of oxytocin on a nitro resin, and Takashima, Merrifield, and du Vigneaud (135) reported the synthesis of desamino oxytocin, also on the nitro resin. In these syntheses the am-

monolysis was done in methanolic ammonia. This general approach is still fraught with difficulties, however, since Beyerman et al. (11) were unable to ammonolyze the oxytocin chain from the regular resin, and Bodanszky and Sheehan (15) obtained a peptide ester when they attempted to synthesize the C-terminal sequence of secretin by solid phase. This latter difficulty was apparently caused by the fact that valine occurs in the C-terminal position of secretin, since this peptide ester was ammonolyzed in solution only with difficulty. More recently, Beyerman succeeded in his oxytocin synthesis (10), and three other laboratories have synthesized oxytocin and analogs on the regular resin (5, 44, 59). Further experiments are needed to delineate the possibilities of this approach and to develop more effective methods of ammonolysis. Results thus far seem to indicate that small peptides may be ammonolyzed readily, but longer ones may be ammonolyzed only in low yield, if at all. Again, the use of a proper swelling solvent for the ammonolysis may greatly improve the situation.

In general, the use of a nitro resin support should favor successful ammonolysis, since the benzyl ester linking the peptide to the nitro resin is activated to some extent for nucleophilic displacement. A nitro resin also offers one solution to the problem of retention of aspartic and glutamic carboxyl groups during ammonolysis. If these carboxyls are protected during the syntheses as benzyl esters, they will be converted to amides during the ammonolysis. In one approach (128), a peptide was synthesized by the diimide method on the nitro resin, and the peptide-resin was then treated with hydrogen bromide in trifluoroacetic acid in the usual cleavage procedure, which removed the benzyl esters of aspartic and glutamic acid residues, but did not cleave the peptide from the resin. (The nitro resin was developed by Merrifield to provide a peptide linkage stable to removal of carbobenzoxy groups by hydrogen bromide in acetic acid.) Subsequent treatment of this peptide-resin with methanolic ammonia removed the peptide as the amide. Since free carboxyl groups are not readily convertible to amides, aspartic and glutamic acids, as well as asparagine and glutamine, could be incorporated at will into peptide amides. An alternative approach is to use the nitrophenyl ester coupling method throughout and to incorporate aspartic and glutamic acids without any ester protecting group on the ω-carboxyls. Such a peptide-resin should be directly ready for ammonolysis. Both these procedures should avoid any risk of converting aspartyl peptides to the β-linkage. It seems that t-butyl esters should also provide ammonia-resistant protection for aspartic and glutamic acids. These esters could be removed by hydrogen fluoride or by hydrogen bromide in trifluoroacetic acid after ammonolysis. However, they are not compatible with t-butyloxycarbonyl α-protecting groups. Another possible route to peptide amides would be to remove the peptide from the resin by transesterification with triethyl amine and methanol, and then to ammonolyze the resulting peptide methyl ester in solution.

Bodanazky and Sheehan (14) reported that hydrazinolysis of a peptide on a nitro resin proceeded satisfactorily, and more recently the regular, nonnitrated resin was used for the successful synthesis of the hydrazides of a tripeptide (45), and hexapeptide (93), and of a group of dansyl proline oligomers containing up to twelve residues (134). As we pointed out earlier, hydrazinolysis should be particularly useful in the solid phase synthesis of peptides that could be further coupled into longer peptides in solution by the azide method, and the hexapeptide hydrazide was indeed prepared for this purpose.

PROTECTING GROUPS FOR SOLID PHASE SYNTHESIS

Protection and deprotection of α-amino groups

Although the original solid phase synthesis of a peptide described by Merrifield used the benzyloxycarbonyl (carbobenzoxy) protecting group for α-amino functions, he later found the t-butyloxycarbonyl protecting group to be so much more satisfactory that nearly all subsequent solid phase syntheses of peptides have used the latter group.

In the original synthesis of a tetrapeptide (71), the carbobenzoxy group was removed at each stage of the synthesis by use of anhydrous hydrogen bromide in acetic acid (Figure 7), which normally cleaves benzyl esters, and would therefore cleave the amino acid from the usual resin support. To prevent this undesired cleavage, Merrifield nitrated the chloromethyl resin before attaching the first amino acid. The nitrobenzyl ester, which resulted when a carbobenzoxy amino acid was esterified to the nitrochloromethyl resin, was found to be stable to the action of hydrogen bromide in acetic acid. The final peptide was cleaved from the resin by saponification. This reaction sequence has the serious disadvantage that the finished peptide must be exposed to alkali, which might cause racemization of some amino acids, and might also cause aspartic acid residues to be converted to β-aspartyl peptide linkages (4, 124). Although no longer routinely used, the nitro resin may be useful for solid phase synthesis where the peptide is to be removed from the resin by ammonolysis or hydrazinolysis (14, 128).

Use of the carbobenzoxy protecting group creates further problems if the synthesis involves serine or threonine. Although in classical peptide synthesis serine and threonine can often be used without the hydroxyl groups being protected during synthesis, in solid phase synthesis these groups must generally be protected. Unless these hydroxyl groups are blocked, the large excess of activated amino acid used to insure complete coupling of each introduced residue will sometimes cause acylation of the hydroxyl by the amino acid. Since the ester bond thus formed is stable to the conditions of the synthesis, a branch may form in the peptide chain, and lengthen in subsequent steps of the synthesis. Benzyl ethers are currently used to protect the hydroxyl groups of serine and

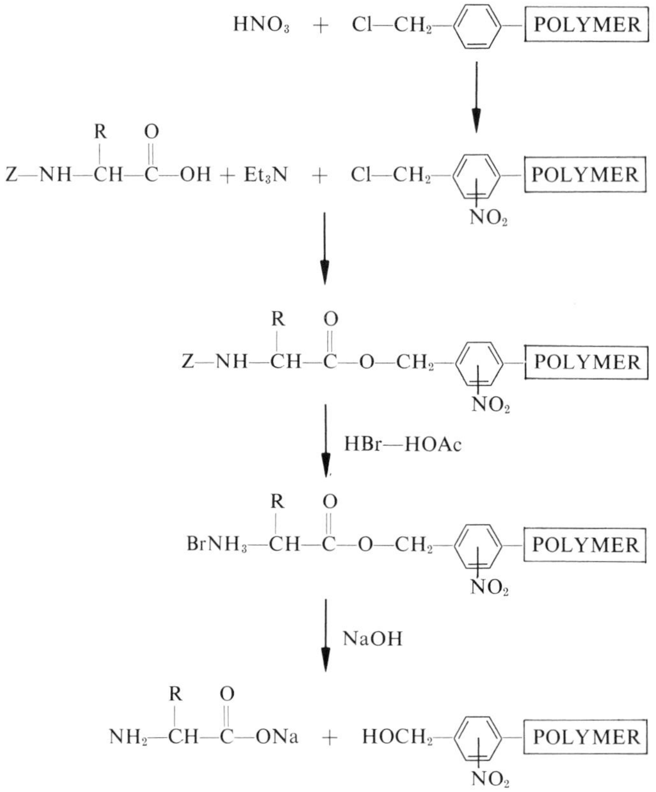

FIGURE 7.
Solid Phase Synthesis with Carbobenzoxy Amino Acids.

threonine in conjunction with t-butyloxycarbonyl amine protecting groups, and are stable to the anhydrous hydrogen chloride used for removal of the t-butyloxycarbonyl group. However, when the carbobenzoxy group is used, the hydrogen bromide in acetic acid used to remove the carbobenzoxy group also removes the benzyl ether and substitutes for it an acetyl group. If saponification is used to remove the peptide from the resin, the acetyl groups will also be removed, but their presence must be reckoned with if other, more desirable methods of cleaving the peptide from the resin are to be applied. Acetylation of serine and threonine residues might also be avoided by using hydrogen bromide in trifluoroacetic acid to remove carbobenzoxy groups at each step, although this procedure has not been used in solid phase synthesis,

and would be quite inconvenient, since the limited solubility of hydrogen bromide in trifluoroacetic acid would require that gaseous hydrogen bromide be bubbled through the resin suspension at each step of the synthesis.

In addition, if the carbobenzoxy protecting group is to be used for the solid phase synthesis of peptides containing aspartic or glutamic acids, the side-chain carboxyl groups should be protected with methyl esters. Methyl esters are stable to hydrogen bromide in acetic acid, but are removed by the saponification used to cleave the peptide from the resin.

At the present time, the t-butyloxycarbonyl group is the standard protection for α-amino functions in solid phase synthesis (see Figure 2). The t-butyloxycarbonyl group can be removed by either anyhdrous hydrogen chloride in an organic solvent or anhydrous trifluoroacetic acid. Neither reagent cleaves benzyl esters. We thus have the difference in stability between peptide-resin bonds and α-amine protecting group bonds that is needed for satisfactory peptide synthesis. A nonnitrated polystyrene-divinylbenzene resin can be used as the carrier, and the finished peptide can be cleaved from the resin by anhydrous hydrogen bromide in trifluoroacetic acid or by anhydrous hydrogen fluoride. Both cleavage methods have been found to give satisfactory results and to avoid the dangers inherent in cleavage by saponification. Protecting groups which are both satisfactory for amino acid side-chain functions and compatible with the t-butyloxycarbonyl group are available, and many peptides have now been synthesized by the solid phase method using these groups.

The t-butyloxycarbonyl amino acids are usually synthesized by the reaction of amino acids with t-butyloxycarbonyl azide (Figure 8), since the corresponding acid chloride, unlike carbobenzoxy chloride, is too unstable for convenient use. The best yields of t-butyloxycarbonyl amino acids are generally obtained by Schnabel's method (110), in which the azide and amino acid react at a controlled alkaline pH in a pH-stat. In the absence of a pH-stat, magnesium oxide, sodium bicarbonate, and triethyl amine have all been used as bases to promote the reaction, and have generally given good yields. A method using dimethyl sulfoxide as the solvent has been developed for the synthesis of t-butyloxycarbonyl derivatives of insoluble or alkali-sensitive amino acids. Another suitable reagent for introduction of the t-butyloxycarbonyl group is t-butyl p-nitrophenyl carbonate (1), although it has not been as widely used as the azide.

The t-amyloxycarbonyl protecting group (106, 107) is altogether analogous to the t-butyloxycarbonyl group in chemical reactions, and is used because the t-amyloxycarbonyl amino acids are less expensive. This is because t-amyloxycarbonyl chloride is sufficiently more stable than t-butyloxycarbonyl chloride that it can be used directly for the synthesis of protected amino acids (Figure 9), without recourse to the much more expensive azide or active ester methods of

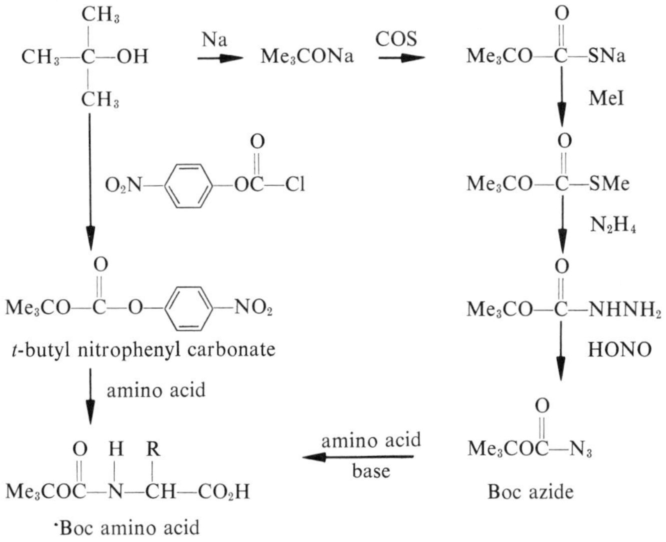

FIGURE 8.
Formation of t-Butyloxycarbonyl Amino Acids.

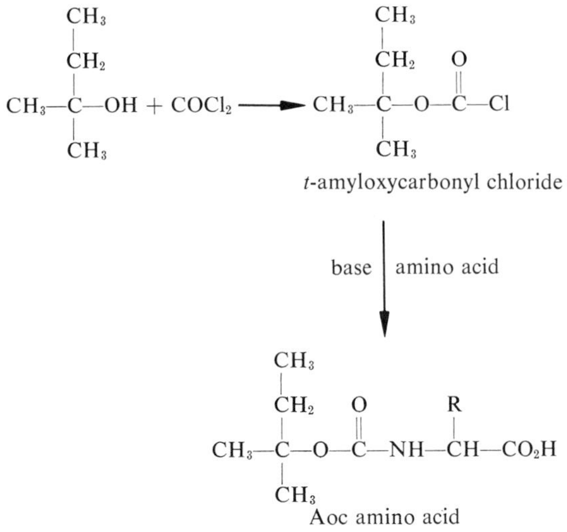

FIGURE 9.
Formation of *t*-Amyloxycarbonyl Amino Acids.

synthesis needed for the *t*-butyloxycarbonyl derivatives. Some *t*-amyloxycarbonyl amino acids are commercially available (see Appendix C), and have been used in solid phase synthesis (103).

An even greater difference in stability can be achieved if the *o*-nitrophenylsulfenyl protecting group is used for α-amino functions (Figure 10). This group can be removed by treatment of the nitrophenylsulfenyl peptide-resin with hydrogen chloride in an inert solvent such as chloroform. Since the nitrophenylsulfenyl group is very labile, only a little more than the theoretical quantity of hydrogen chloride is needed in practice. Najjar and Merrifield used this technique to synthesize the octadecapeptide bradykininyl-bradykinin (88). A further possibility for the removal of nitrophenylsulfenyl groups lies in the use of thiol compounds. Kessler and Iselin (45) have used thioacetamide to remove nitrophenylsulfenyl groups in solid phase synthesis, and disulfide formation by *o*-nitrothiophenol (145) should in principle be applicable to solid phase. These reagents should be particularly useful in the presence of tryptophan residues or acid-labile groups such as *t*-butyl esters or ethers. When nitrophenylsulfenyl amino acids are deprotected with hydrogen chloride, the protecting group is converted to nitrophenylsulfenyl chloride, which alkylates tryptophan irreversibly in acid media.

The nitrophenylsulfenyl amino acids are slightly less convenient to use than other protected amino acids, since, because of the instability of the free acids, they must be stored as salts (dicyclohexyl amine salts have generally been used). Before these derivatives can be used in coupling reactions, they must be liberated from the salt by very careful acid treatment. This operation is not only inconvenient and time-consuming, but also inherently hazardous because of the extreme acid lability of the nitrophenylsulfenyl group. These added inconveniences have kept these derivatives from being customarily chosen for solid phase synthesis, but they are very useful for certain special applications.

The most recent advance in labile protecting groups for solid phase synthesis is the introduction of the 2-(*p*-biphenylyl)-2-propyloxycarbonyl protecting group, which has the structure

$$C_6H_5-C_6H_4-C(CH_3)_2-O-\overset{O}{\overset{\|}{C}}-.$$

This protecting group, in which a *p*-biphenylyl radical has been substituted for one of the methyls in the *t*-butyloxycarbonyl protecting group, is about two thousand times as sensitive as the latter to acidic cleavage. Sieber and Iselin, who introduced this group, used it to protect α-amino groups in the solid phase synthesis of a lysine-containing tetrapeptide. They blocked the ϵ-amino group of lysine with the t-butyloxycarbonyl group, which was stable to the 90-minute treatment with 75 per cent trichloroacetic acid they used to deprotect the α-amino groups.*

The great acid lability of this new protecting group is bought at the cost of several disadvantages. The protecting group must be introduced into amino acids as the azide (as the t-butyloxycarbonyl group must), making for a

tedious and expensive synthesis. The derivatives are so labile to acid that they must be stored as amine salts, and so make necessary a treacherous conversion to the acid immediately before use, as do o-nitrophenylsulfenyl derivatives. In addition, the protecting group is so bulky that the derivatives have a very low weight efficiency, and may cause steric hindrance in some coupling reactions. However, offsetting these disadvantages, the extreme ease with which this group can be removed would allow it to be used for the synthesis of lysine-containing peptides without any risk whatever of partly removing ϵ-carbobenzoxy groups (see p. 20). In addition, since the mild acidolysis used to remove this group does not produce an alkylating agent, which the acidolysis of o-nitrophenylsulfenyl groups does (see p. 49), this

---

*P. Sieber and B. Iselin, *Helv. Chim. Acta*, **51**, 622 (1968).

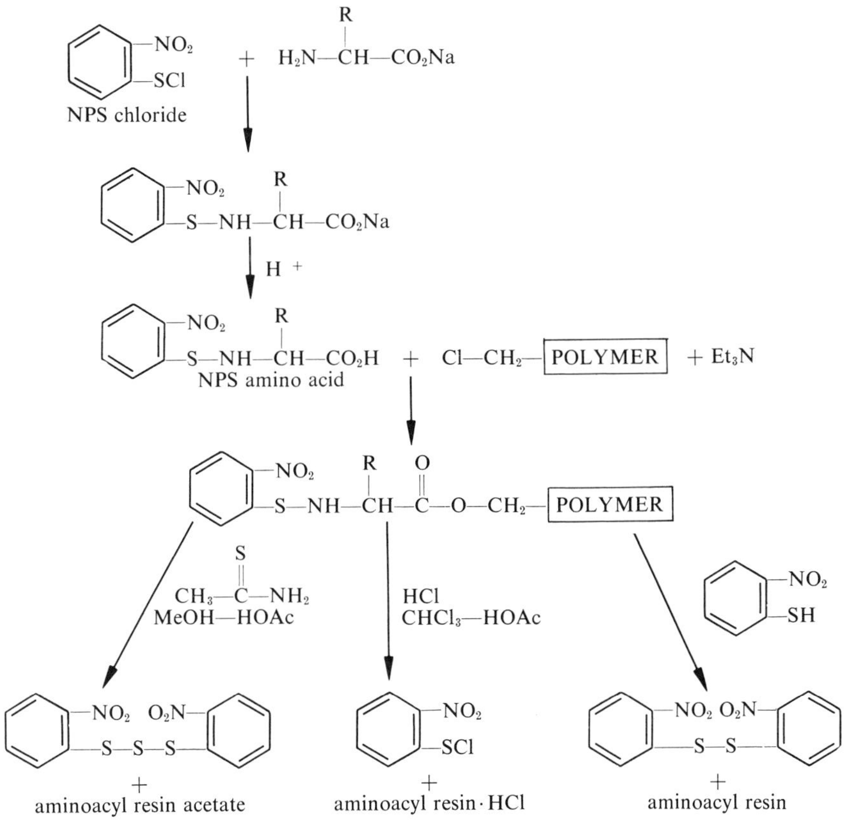

FIGURE 10.
The Nitrophenylsulfenyl Protecting Group.

derivative should be quite satisfactory for synthesis of tryptophan-containing peptides. Further work will be needed to evaluate the group's usefulness completely.

In his synthesis of bradykinin (72), the first peptide made by solid phase using *t*-butyloxycarbonyl amino acids, Merrifield used 1 molar hydrogen chloride in anhydrous acetic acid to remove these protecting groups. This reagent has subsequently been used to synthesize many peptides. However, several syntheses produced evidence that the peptide chain was terminated on the resin because the α-amino group was masked by some stable blocking group (128). The most logical explanation for this undesired side reaction was that some acetic acid had been carried over from the deprotection step to the coupling step, where it was activated by diimide to a derivative which acetylated a certain fraction of the peptide chains. To overcome this difficulty, peroxide-free dioxane was introduced as a solvent for the hydrogen chloride. This reagent eliminated the acetylation, and is now widely used for solid phase synthesis. At certain stages of the synthesis of the heptadecapeptide angiotensinyl-bradykinin, protecting groups could not be satisfactorily removed with hydrogen chloride in acetic acid, whereas hydrogen chloride in dioxane allowed the synthesis to proceed satisfactorily (75). In diimide-mediated couplings, the presence of formic acid in dimethylformamide might also cause termination of peptide chains; all dimethylformamide used as a solvent for coupling reactions should therefore be scrupulously purified.

With this change to dioxane as the solvent in deprotection steps, the hydrogen chloride concentration had to be increased to 4 molar to insure complete removal of *t*-butyloxycarbonyl groups within the 30-minute reaction time desired for this step. In dioxane, a much more basic solvent than acetic acid, much of the hydrogen chloride is presumably bound with the solvent as an oxonium salt. The *t*-butyloxycarbonyl derivatives of various amino acids on the resin support were found to vary widely in their susceptibility to cleavage by hydrogen chloride in dioxane, some being removed by 2 molar acid in 10 minutes, others requiring the full-strength reagent for 30 minutes. Since the reagent is always somewhat diluted by the solvent already present in the resin, complete removal of resistant *t*-butyloxycarbonyl groups can be insured by prewashing the resin with the hydrogen chloride in dioxane, and following with the standard 30-minute deprotection reaction.

One concern in the use of the dioxane solvent for deprotection has been possible oxidative degradation of sensitive amino acid residues by peroxides, which accumulate in the reagent if it is left standing. Although alumina treatment is used to remove peroxides already present in the dioxane before the hydrogen chloride reagent is prepared, additional peroxides are formed if the reagent is allowed to stand for some days or weeks. However, there is no definite evidence yet that these peroxides have any deleterious effects.

Since oxidizing agents in an acidic medium would create problems in the synthesis of tryptophan peptides, dioxane has thus far been avoided in such syntheses. With hydrogen chloride in acetic acid as the reagent, solid phase synthesis of tryptophan peptides has been successful if the deprotection was carried out at reduced temperature or if a reducing agent was present during the acidic stages of the synthesis (see pp. 48–49).

Anhydrous trifluoroacetic acid has frequently been used to remove *t*-butyloxycarbonyl groups in classical peptide synthesis, and is logically applicable to solid phase synthesis. One interesting recent application of trifluoroacetic acid cleavage of *t*-butyloxycarbonyl groups led to the solution of a problem in the solid phase synthesis of an oxytocin analog (135). Glutamine has been successfully introduced into several peptides by solid phase synthesis, but incorporation of glutamine into a peptide-resin has sometimes caused termination of peptide chains (128, 135), most probably because of cyclization of the N-terminal glutamine to a pyroglutamic acid residue in the anhydrous hydrogen chloride medium used to remove the *t*-butyloxycarbonyl protecting group from the glutamine. Merrifield reasoned that, since trifluoroacetic acid had prevented a similar undesired cyclization of N-terminal glutamine residues in the Edman degradation, it might be useful in this situation also; when anhydrous trifluoroacetic acid was used to remove the *t*-butyloxycarbonyl group from the glutamine residue, the next coupling reaction proceeded normally.

Protection and deprotection of side-chain functional groups

In solid phase synthesis, as in peptide synthesis by classical methods, side-chain functional groups of the trifunctional amino acids must be protected during the synthetic procedures. The protecting groups used for this purpose must be stable to all reagents used for removal of α-amine blocking groups during the synthesis, and must be removable at the end of the synthesis by reagents which will not cleave peptide bonds or modify any amino acid residues. This problem is sometimes aggravated in the solid phase method by the need to use excess activated amino acid during each coupling reaction. Suitable protecting groups compatible with the solid phase method are available for all the trifunctional amino acids.

Arginine. The protecting group chosen for the guanidine function of arginine will depend on the nature of the peptide being synthesized. In general, when peptides are to be cleaved from the resin support by hydrogen bromide in trifluoroacetic acid, this choice will be determined by whether there is cysteine in the peptide or not. When cysteine is absent, nitroarginine is the most commonly used derivative, and many arginine-containing peptides have been synthesized by solid phase in this way. After the cleavage of the peptide from the resin, the nitroarginine is hydrogenolyzed to arginine

in the peptide by shaking a solution of the peptide with a palladium catalyst in a hydrogen atmosphere.

Catalytic hydrogenolysis usually fails with peptides containing cysteine or methionine, since the sulfur poisons the catalyst. At least one successful hydrogenolysis of nitroarginine (over freshly prepared palladium black) in a methionine-containing peptide has been reported, however (74), and at least one catalyst, palladium oxide on barium sulfate, has been reported to function satisfactorily in the presence of cysteine (51). The formation of peptides containing partial reduction products of nitroarginine (43) is one possible complication in the use of this procedure. If the peptide contains cysteine (protected as the S-benzyl derivative), arginine has generally been introduced as the guanidino-tosyl derivative, and protecting groups are then removed from both residues by treatment of the cleaved peptide with sodium in liquid ammonia. This latter procedure is hazardous, however, especially for proline-containing peptides (8, 80). When anhydrous hydrogen fluoride is used for simultaneous cleavage and deprotection of peptides, arginine should be introduced as nitroarginine, which is readily cleaved to arginine by this reagent (106).

Several arginine-containing peptides have been synthesized by classical methods in solution without any protecting group on the guanidine (114). The guanidine group, because of its very high *p*K, remains protonated throughout the usual coupling reactions, and this protonation has been found to provide sufficient protection for the group. One peptide has been synthesized by solid phase using α-*t*-butyloxycarbonyl arginine (55). However, other attempts to couple guanidine-unprotected arginine to a resin or peptide-resin were unsuccessful (66). Further work is needed to clarify this point.

Lysine. The carbobenzoxy group has proved to be suitable for protection of the ϵ-amino group of lysine in solid phase synthesis. It is compatible with the use of either *t*-butyloxycarbonyl or nitrophenylsulfenyl groups and is readily removed by hydrogen bromide in trifluoroacetic acid, liquid hydrogen fluoride, or sodium in liquid ammonia. There has been a suggestion that the ε-carbobenzoxy group may have been partially cleaved by the hydrogen chloride in acetic acid used in the normal deprotection step during the synthesis of a group of lysine oligomers (9). However, a similar synthetic project in another laboratory yielded the desired product with no evidence of such partial deprotection (29), and long peptides containing lysine have been synthesized with no evidence of branching on the lysine (62). The o-nitrophenylsulfenyl (see p. 17) and 2-(p-biphenylyl)-2-propyloxycarbonyl (see p. 17) protecting groups are much more readily removed from α-amino groups than the t-butyloxycarbonyl group is, and use of one of them should avoid all risk of partly deprotecting the lysine ε-amino groups.

The trifluoroacetyl protecting group has also been successfully used for the ε-amino group of lysine in solid phase synthesis (93). This group is removed from the finished peptide by treatment with 1 molar piperidine at 0° for one or two hours, though the removal may sometimes be very slow.

Histidine. A completely suitable protecting group for the imidazole ring of histidine in solid phase synthesis has not yet been described. Solid phase syntheses of peptides incorporating this amino acid have used the *im*-N-benzyl protecting group, and deprotection has been by catalytic hydrogenolysis or sodium in liquid ammonia. Neither of these deprotection methods is completely satisfactory, however. Catalytic hydrogenolysis over palladium catalysts of benzyl histidine in peptides is often a slow reaction, requiring up to 72 hours for completion, and sometimes, apparently because of steric hindrance in the peptide structure, the debenzylation fails completely (50). Reduction by sodium in liquid ammonia is a very drastic treatment, and most peptide chemists would prefer not to use it. The 1-benzyloxycarbonyl-amino-2,2,2-trifluoroethyl protecting group recently described by Weygand et al. (141) would appear to be compatible with the t-butyloxycarbonyl or nitrophenylsulfenyl α-amine protecting groups (Figure 11), although no reports of its use in solid phase have appeared. It should be stable to the reagents used to remove either of the latter two groups, and should itself be readily cleaved by hydrogen bromide in trifluoroacetic acid or by hydrogen fluoride.

The recent discovery that imidazole-dinitrophenyl groups can be readily cleaved from histidine by thiols at pH 8 and room temperature (119) offers great promise for a convenient protecting group for histidine in solid phase synthesis (Figure 12). Preliminary data indicate that this group can be used satisfactorily in solid phase synthesis (57).

One brief report (55) has indicated that it may be possible to carry out solid phase synthesis of histidine peptides without a protecting group on the imidazole.

Aspartic and glutamic acids. The ω-carboxyl groups of these amino acids have been satisfactorily protected in solid phase work as benzyl esters, which are removed by all the common procedures for deblocking side-chain functions. In one study where it was desired to have the glutamic carboxyl remain protected until after the peptide had been cleaved from the resin (143), the glutamic acid was introduced into the peptide as t-butyloxycarbonylglutamic acid γ-p-nitrobenzyl ester. This ester is stable to hydrogen bromide in trifluoroacetic acid, and was removed later by hydrogenolysis. Because of the insolubility of γ-p-nitrobenzyl glutamate, the synthesis of this derivative presented a problem which was solved by developing a new method for the introduction of the t-butyloxycarbonyl group, using dimethyl sulfoxide as the solvent (see p. 29).

Cystine. All solid phase syntheses of cysteine peptides reported so far have used α-t-butyloxycarbonyl-S-benzyl cysteine to intro-

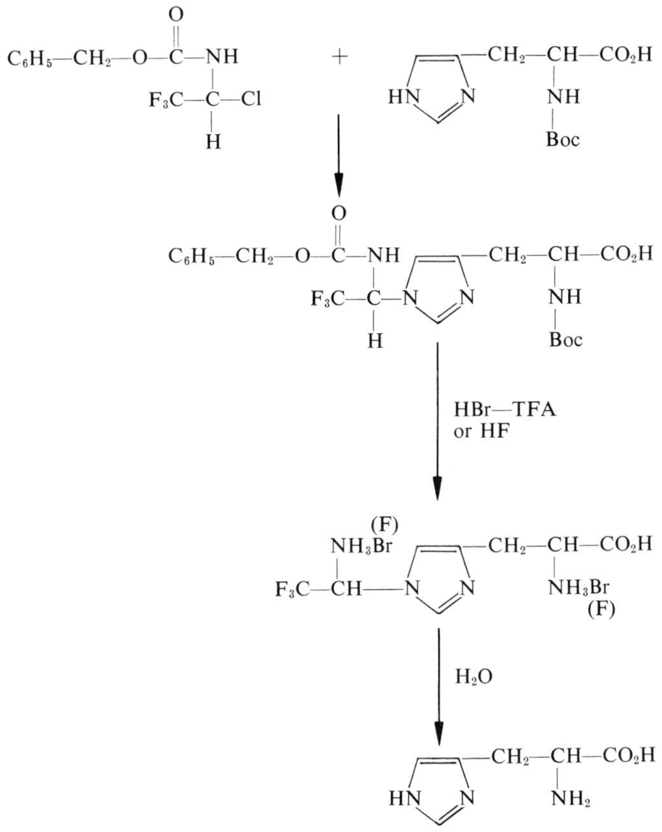

FIGURE 11.
The Weygand Protecting Group for Histidine.

duce this amino acid. This group can be removed satisfactorily only by sodium in liquid ammonia, which must be used under carefully controlled conditions (80). With anhydrous hydrogen fluoride, the removal of S-benzyl groups requires conditions which may promote N–O or N–S migration of acyl groups. To overcome this difficulty, Sakakibara (106) has used S-p-methoxybenzyl cysteine, from which the protecting group can be removed readily by anhydrous hydrogen fluoride, and which will probably prove to be ideal for protection of cysteine residues.

When anhydrous hydrogen fluoride or hydrogen bromide in trifluoroacetic acid is used to remove carbobenzoxy groups or benzyl esters or ethers, the benzyl group is removed as benzyl fluoride or bromide, respectively. To insure complete removal of the benzyl groups from the cysteine and to prevent benzylation of methionine and tyrosine, a suitable scavenger must be present to react with the benzyl halide formed. To protect cysteine and methionine residues, a large excess of ethyl methyl sulfide or diethyl phosphite (32) or of free methionine (62) has been used with hydrogen bromide in trifluoroacetic acid, and anisole has been used to protect all sensitive amino acids during hydrogen fluoride cleavage.

Methionine. In the limited work reported so far, methionine has been used in solid phase synthesis without protection of the thioether (74). A suitable scavenger must be used in the cleavage reaction to prevent conversion of

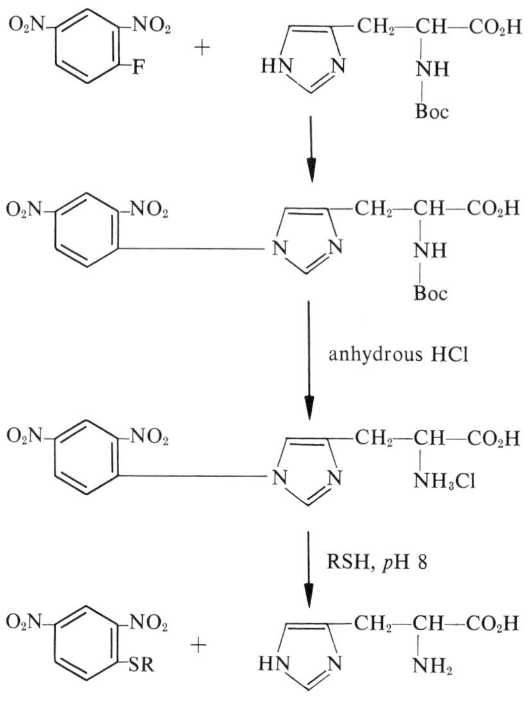

FIGURE 12.
Use of DNP Histidine.

methionine to the benzylsulfonium derivative, but protection of methionine by such a scavenger has not always been completely successful (42). Hydrogenolysis of other protecting groups in methionine-containing peptides may present problems. Nitroarginine was successfully hydrogenolyzed to arginine in methionyl-lysyl-bradykinin (74), but has presented difficulties in other syntheses (69). Sodium in liquid ammonia should not be used for cleavage unless no other procedure is feasible.

Serine and threonine. For completely satisfactory use of these amino acids in solid phase synthesis, their hydroxyl groups must be protected, for which purpose benzyl ethers have worked well. O-benzylserine has been used throughout the development of the solid phase method. Until very recently, however, O-benzylthreonine was not readily available, and threonine has been introduced into peptides by the solid phase method without any protection of the hydroxyl group, usually with satisfactory results. However, during several syntheses (130, 131), by-products having a chain branch attached to the threonine hydroxyl were formed (Figure 13). This undesired side-reaction was evidently due to the excess (2.5 times the theoretical amount) of activated amino acid present during the coupling reactions. A practicable synthesis of O-benzylthreonine has now been developed (84), and the use of α-t-butyl-oxycarbonyl-O-benzylthreonine in solid phase synthesis has completely eliminated the problem of chain branching on threonine.

One further difficulty has been encountered in synthesizing certain threonine and serine peptides that also contain glutamic or aspartic acids (75, 143). When a glutamic or aspartic acid residue is so situated in a peptide sequence that its side-chain carboxyl group is held close

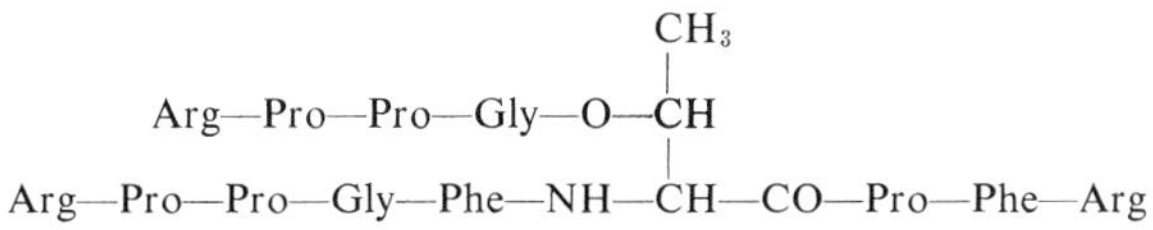

$$\text{Arg—Pro—Pro—Gly—O—}\overset{\displaystyle \overset{CH_3}{|}}{\underset{\displaystyle |}{CH}}$$

$$\text{Arg—Pro—Pro—Gly—Phe—NH—CH—CO—Pro—Phe—Arg}$$

FIGURE 13.
Branched Peptide Formed During the Synthesis of 6-Threonine Bradykinin.

to the free hydroxyl of a threonine or serine residue, these residues may form a cyclic ester under dehydrating conditions, such as exist in the anhydrous acid media used to cleave peptides from the resin support. This situation is not peculiar to the solid phase method, and would be expected to arise if the same peptides were made by classical methods in solution. In one case where this side reaction was observed (Figure 14), formation of the undesired product was eliminated by using for glutamic acid a *p*-nitrobenzyl ester, which was not cleaved by the hydrogen bromide in trifluoroacetic acid used to cleave the peptide from the resin. This ester was removed from the glutamic acid by subsequent hydrogenolysis in an aqueous medium, which inhibited esterification. In any event, such esters were apparently opened by very mild base treatment, such as chromatography in a pyridine-collidine buffer (143). This presumed esterification has not as yet been reported to occur in peptides cleaved from the resin by anhydrous hydrogen fluoride, although this gap in information may reflect lack of experience with the medium rather than any chemical difference.

Tyrosine. The hydroxyl group of tyrosine has been protected in solid phase synthesis as a benzyl ether, which is readily removed by hydrogen bromide in trifluoroacetic acid or by hydrogenolysis. O-benzyl tyrosine is relatively stable to anhydrous hydrogen fluoride (106), so that the conditions needed for cleavage (more than an hour at 0°) are so vigorous as to cause concern for the stability of the peptide. Sakakibara has used O-*t*-butyl tyrosine in conjunction with N-*t*-amyloxycarbonyl groups, which were removed with anhydrous trifluoroacetic acid. It may well be that for hydrogen fluoride cleavage, a *p*-methoxybenzyl ether will prove ideal. In any case, when anhydrous hydrogen fluoride or hydrogen bromide in trifluoroacetic acid is used for removal of benzyl esters or ethers or of carbobenzoxy groups from tyrosine-containing peptides, a suitable scavenger must be present to prevent benzylation of the tyrosine. One solid phase synthesis (10) successfully used tyrosine without protection of the hydroxyl group.

COUPLING REACTIONS IN SOLID PHASE SYNTHESIS

Most of the coupling reactions commonly used in classical peptide synthesis in solution should in principle be applicable to solid phase synthesis, and several have already been so used. Dicyclohexylcarbodiimide is the most widely used coupling agent in solid phase peptide synthesis. Except for asparagine and glutamine, all the common amino acids have been success-

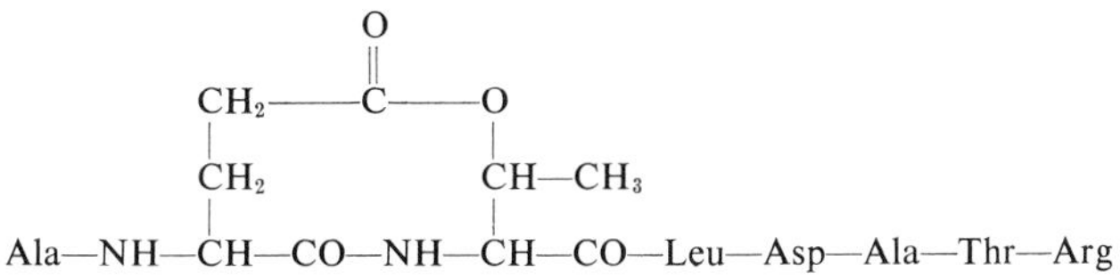

$$\overset{\displaystyle CH_2—\overset{\displaystyle \overset{O}{\|}}{C}—O}{\underset{\displaystyle \underset{\displaystyle \text{Ala—NH—CH—CO—NH—CH—CO—Leu—Asp—Ala—Thr—Arg}}{|}}{\underset{CH_2}{|}\quad \underset{CH—CH_3}{|}}}$$

FIGURE 14.
Possible Structure of a Byproduct Formed in the Synthesis of a TMV Peptide.

fully introduced into peptides of many different lengths by means of this reagent. There have been no reports of racemization of *t*-butyloxy-carbonyl or *o*-nitrophenylsulfenyl amino acids in diimide-mediated solid phase coupling reactions. The reagent is commercially available, inexpensive, and convenient to use, and promotes very rapid coupling. These advantages have been responsible for its wide application to solid phase, in spite of certain cautions and limitations associated with its use.

The ω-amide functions of asparagine and glutamine may be dehydrated to nitriles by diimides during the coupling reaction (16), and a certain proportion of these ω-cyano derivatives may thus be permanently incorporated into the peptide chain. This side reaction has precluded the use of diimides for the incorporation of glutamine and asparagine residues in solid phase synthesis, since there is no way that these by-products may be conveniently removed. This problem has been successfully overcome by using *p*-nitrophenyl esters to introduce these amino acids into peptide chains. Suitable conditions for these reactions are discussed below.

An undersirable side-reaction in the coupling of all amino acids by means of diimide reagents is rearrangement of the active intermediate to the unreactive acyl urea (Figure 15), which reduces the amount of activated amino acid available for reactions and necessitates the use of an excess of protected amino acid and diimide at each step. The fraction of the reactants lost at each step by this side-reaction depends on the structure of the amino acid being activated, the structure of the amine component of the reaction (the last-introduced amino acid), the solvent, and the concentration of the reactants during the reaction. Bulky amino acid residues, in either the activated component or the amine component, slow down the reaction rate and allow the activated complex more time to rearrange to the undesired acyl urea. The rate of rearrangement is greatly affected by the nature of the solvent, being faster in solvents of high polarity. The control of these factors is well-exemplified by Merrifield's experience in

his synthesis of bradykinin (72). He found that when dimethylformamide was the reaction medium, all the amino acids of bradykinin could be completely coupled by the use of two to four equivalents of each amino acid (and of dicyclohexylcarbodiimide) except proline, of which eight equivalents were required. In contrast, when dichloromethane (methylene chloride) was the solvent, 1.5 equivalents of each amino acid was adequate, which is why dichloromethane is used for diimide-mediated coupling reactions whenever possible. As a general routine, 2.5 equivalents of each amino acid and diimide are used in order to provide a greater margin of safety. Three amino acids, the *t*-butyloxycarbonyl derivatives of nitro-arginine, tryptophan, and *im*-benzylhistidine, do not dissolve well enough in dichloromethane to allow exclusive use of it. Instead, these protected amino acids are dissolved in the minimum amount necessary of purified dimethylformamide, and the solution is then made up to the desired volume with dichloromethane.

The volume of solvent used in coupling reactions is usually close to the minimum amount needed to suspend the resin as a slurry in the reaction vessel and to allow for proper mixing. This high concentration promotes the desired coupling reaction at the expense of the rearrangement to the acyl urea, which is intramolecular and proceeds at a fixed rate (for any given amino acid, solvent, and temperature) regardless of concentration, whereas the coupling reaction is bimolecular and proceeds faster when the concentration is high. Since the concentration of reactive groups on the resin is fixed, concentration can be effectively increased only by lowering the volume of the solvent which suspends the resin and dissolves the soluble reactant. At the present time, the effect of temperature on the ratio between the rearrangement and coupling rates has not been adequately investigated.

Users of dicyclohexylcarbodiimide should be reminded that it is a potent contact allergen, and that some people have experienced severe reactions to repeated skin contact. Scrupulous

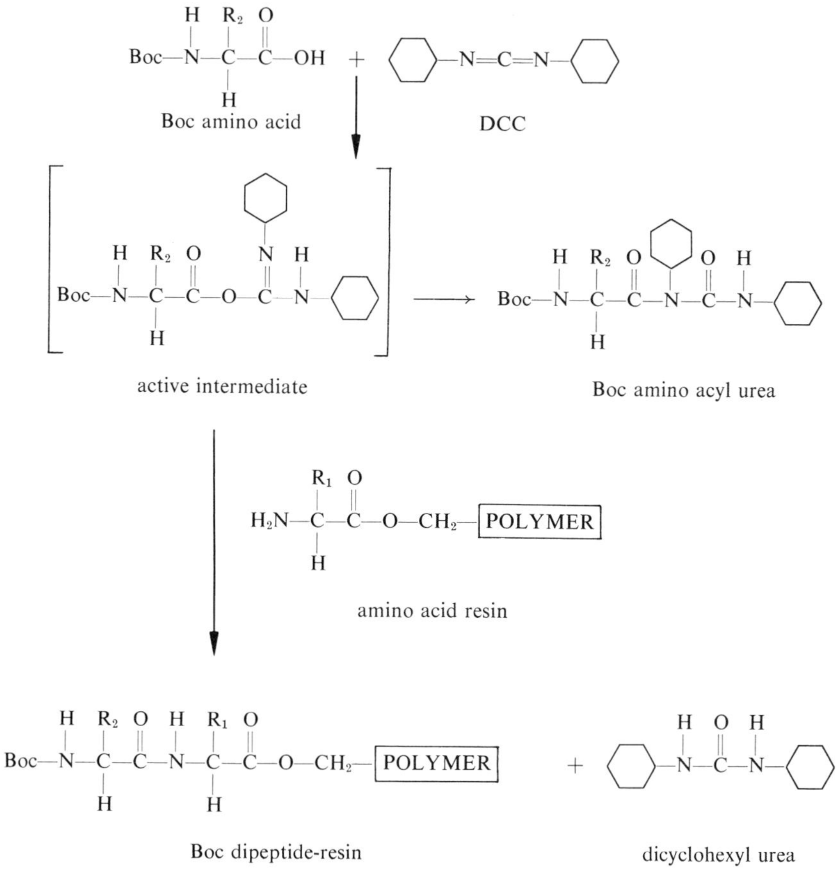

FIGURE 15.
Acyl Urea Formation in Diimide Reactions.

cleanliness must be observed in all areas where the reagent is used, especially in areas around balances. Small bits of diimide carelessly left on balance tables may cause great discomfort to sensitized persons who subsequently use the area. Sensitive persons should routinely wear disposable plastic gloves when handling the reagent.

Active esters of a variety of amino acids have now been used successfully in solid phase synthesis [(14); Figure 16]. As we mentioned above, p-nitrophenyl esters of t-butyloxycarbonyl asparagine and glutamine are routinely used to introduce these residues into peptides in order to avoid the diimide-induced dehydration of the amide to the nitrile. Nitrophenyl esters have also been used exclusively for the synthesis of several peptides (15), including the entire A-chain of insulin (39). The coupling reactions of these esters are generally slower than diimide-mediated couplings. In the Merrifield laboratory, satisfactory coupling of several amino acid nitrophenyl esters has been obtained with four equivalents of the active ester and a reaction time of four hours, in contrast to the routine use of 2.5 equivalents of reactants and a coupling time of two hours for diimide-mediated reactions. Other investigators have sometimes found it necessary to use even more time. One possible advantage of active esters is that the excess reagent, necessary to promote complete coupling within a reasonable time, should in principle be recoverable from the mixture at the end of the reaction. Where the cost of the reagents is a limitation, this might possibly be a deciding factor, since with the diimide reactions,

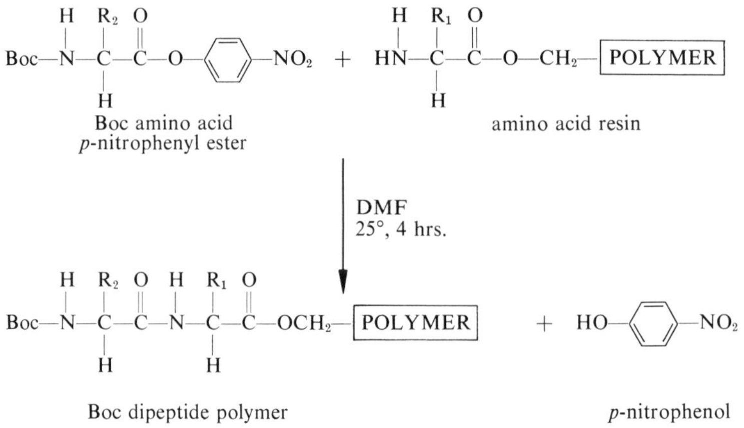

FIGURE 16.
Solid Phase Synthesis with Active Esters.

the excess amino acid is presumably lost as the acyl urea. Beyerman *et al.* (10, 11) have used nitrophenyl esters in the presence of a 1,2,4-triazole catalyst for the solid phase synthesis of oxytocin. Nitrophenyl esters couple satisfactorily only in a dimethylformamide solvent. The dimethylformamide used for this purpose must be carefully purified, since any dimethyl amine present could react with the active ester.

Other active esters have so far been less promising. In a bradykinin synthesis, N-hydroxysuccinimide esters were found to give less satisfactory results than diimide couplings (128). The N-hydroxysuccinimide ester of a dipeptide has been used to lengthen a peptide chain by two amino acids at one step (140). There is one brief report of the use of dicyclohexylcarbodiimide in the presence of N-hydroxysuccinimide (140). Other active esters, the trichloro-

phenyl and pentachlorophenyl esters of nitrophenylsulfenyl amino acids, were reported to give unsatisfactory results in solid phase (11).

Other coupling agents have been used even less frequently. Woodward's reagent (N-ethyl-5-phenylisoxazolium-3'-sulfonate) has been used for the solid phase synthesis of an angiotensin analog (17). Mixed anhydrides have been used to synthesize a tripeptide (117) and a depsipeptide (118), and in a synthesis involving ε-aminocaproic acid (102). At least one amino acid has been coupled to a peptide-resin by the azide method (142). Although Woodward's reagent may prove useful for solid phase work, the other two methods appear impractical for routine syntheses because of the additional work necessary to prepare the active intermediates.

2

LABORATORY TECHNIQUES IN SOLID PHASE PEPTIDE SYNTHESIS

STARTING MATERIALS

Preparation of the resin

Preparation of chloromethyl resin (73). Swell 50 g of resin beads (polystyrene that has been copolymerized with 2% divinylbenzene; see Appendix C, item 1) by stirring at 25° for 1 hour in 200 ml of $CHCl_3$ in a three-neck $ round-bottom flask, then cool it to 0°. Add a cold solution of 3.8 ml anhydrous $SnCl_4$ in 100 ml of chloromethyl methyl ether from a dropping funnel, while stirring. Continue stirring for 30 min. at 0°. Filter the mixture on a fritted glass Buchner funnel, and wash with 1 liter of 3 parts dioxane to 1 part water, then with 1 liter of 3 parts dioxane to 1 part 3 N HCl, allowing several brief periods for the wash solvent to soak into the beads. Wash the beads thoroughly with dioxane, with water, and with methanol, allowing time for each solvent to penetrate the beads. Dry the resin overnight over $CaCl_2$ under high vacuum.

To determine the degree of chloromethylation, heat an aliquot of the resin (200 mg) in 3 ml pyridine in a test tube for 2 hours at 100°. Transfer the mixture quantitatively to a 125-ml Erlenmeyer flask with 30 ml of 50% HOAc, and add 5 ml of concentrated HNO_3. Analyze the chloride by the modified Volhard method (see

p. 55), omitting the addition of nitric acid and adding only 5 ml of $AgNO_3$ (0.1 N). These conditions for chloromethylation have yielded 0.9 to 2.0 millimoles of Cl per g of resin. The degree of chloromethylation can be controlled by changing the amount of $SnCl_4$ used or the time and temperature of the reaction.

Preparation of nitrochloromethyl resin (71). Slowly add 50 g of chloromethyl resin (1 to 2 millimoles of Cl per g of resin), while stirring, to a beaker containing 500 ml of fuming nitric acid (90% HNO_3, sp. gr. 1.5) prechilled in an ice-salt bath to 0°. Continue stirring at 0° for 1 hour. Pour the mixture onto crushed ice. After the ice melts, filter the resin on a coarse fritted glass Buchner funnel, and wash successively with water, dioxane, and methanol. Dry the resin under vacuum. These conditions have yielded 6.4 millimoles NO_2 group per g of resin, as estimated by Dumas nitrogen analysis. This degree of substitution represents approximately one NO_2 group per aromatic ring.

Preparation of hydroxymethyl resin (83). Cover chloromethyl resin (1 to 2 millimoles of Cl per g of resin; 1 equiv. Cl) and potassium acetate (1.1 equiv.) with methyl cellosolve (approximately 6 ml per g of resin) and heat in an oil bath at 125° to 135° for 24 hours. The reaction is carried out in a ⊺ 24/40 round-bottom flask fitted with a 500-mm water condenser carrying a CaCl₂ drying tube. Filter the acetoxy resin which results from this procedure and wash thoroughly with water and with methanol. The yield of acetoxy resin is measured by titration of chloride in the combined filtrate and wash (see p. 55). This procedure usually gives essentially complete conversion to the acetoxy form. Saponify the acetylated resin by stirring for 48 hours at room temperature with 25 ml per g of resin of a mixture of 2 vols dioxane and one vol 0.5 N NaOH. At least 2 equiv. of NaOH should be used for each equiv. of acetoxy groups. Filter the resin, wash with water and then methanol, and dry. The degree of saponification to the hydroxymethyl resin is estimated by back-titration of the aqueous wash with standard HCl. This series of reactions can also be monitored qualitatively by infrared spectroscopy (26, 54). KBr pellets may be made of the polymer beads directly.

Preparation of Boc
amino acids

Synthesis of Boc amino acids in a pH-stat:
The Schnabel method (110). Suspend 0.05 mole of the amino acid and 0.055 mole of Boc azide in 10 ml of water and 10 ml of dioxane, and place in the vessel of a pH-stat (autotitrator). Fill the reservoir of the pH-stat with 4 N NaOH. Advance the pH control of the instrument to the point where continued uptake of base indicates that the reaction is proceeding at a reasonable rate. A few amino acids will react at pH 8.5, and most at pH 9.8; a few require pH 10.2 for a reasonable rate of reaction. The reaction is usually complete in a few hours, although the reaction with certain amino acids is quite sluggish and may require more than 24 hours. Amino acid derivatives containing alkali-labile groups (e.g., esters and amides of aspartic and glutamic acids) should be treated with caution; the reaction should be carried out at the lowest

pH practical. With these derivatives, purer products will probably be obtained by use of the dimethyl sulfoxide procedure (see p. 29).

The end of the reaction is indicated by cessation of base uptake. Extract the solution 3 times with ether to remove unreacted azide. Chill the aqueous phase in ice, acidify with solid citric acid to pH 3, and extract 3 times with ethyl acetate. Certain Boc amino acids (serine, threonine) are quite soluble in water and can not be satisfactorily extracted by the ethyl acetate; if using them, saturate the aqueous phase with NaCl before the extraction. A recent report (70) indicates that better yields may be obtained if the chilled reaction mixture is acidified to pH 2 with HCl in a pH-stat, then extracted in the usual way with ethyl acetate.

Wash the ethyl acetate extract 3 times with small portions of water (saturated NaCl solution for water-soluble derivatives), dry over MgSO₄, and evaporate under reduced pressure. Most Boc amino acids can be crystallized from EtOAc-hexane. Of the commonly used derivatives, Boc methionine and α-Boc-ε-Z-lysine usually fail to crystallize, and are frequently crystallized as dicylcohexylamine salts, but using the latter introduces an extra recovery step before the Boc amino acids can be used in synthesis, and is not recommended.

Boc-*im*-Bzl-His is a zwitterion and cannot be extracted from aqueous acid. For it, adjust the reaction mixture to pH 6.0 with solid citric acid and concentrate under reduced pressure until crystallization begins. Chill the suspension for several hours and filter to remove the product.

Purity of the Boc amino acids is most conveniently assessed by TLC (see pp. 58–60). The Boc group is removed from the derivatives by exposure to HCl vapor after development of the plates in the appropriate solvent; the ninhydrin spray can then be used. Boc amino acids, if pure, are stable at room temperature for long periods of time, but any traces of acid remaining in them will promote cleavage of the Boc group and accumulation of free amino acid. A rough measure of whether there is free amino acid is the solubility of the Boc derivative in CH₂Cl₂; most Boc derivatives (except those of nitroarginine, tosylarginine, *im*-Bzl histidine, and tryptophan) are soluble to the extent of 1 g in 10 ml. An undissolved residue usually indicates presence of free amino acid, which should be removed by filtration. It is especially important that free amino acids not be present in the Boc derivatives, since they will cause undesirable side reactions in the synthesis.

The greatest difficulty is encountered with Boc glutamic acid γ-benzyl ester, since the Boc glutamic acid is almost impossible to separate by precipitation or crystallization. The dimethyl sulfoxide method of synthesis (see below) is preferred for this derivative. The following CCD was developed (78) to purify this derivative:

For the solvent, use: *n*-butanol, 600 ml; pyridine, 100 ml; acetic acid, 10 ml; water, 850 ml.

Set up a CCD system of 7 separatory funnels. For 21 g of crude material, use 175 ml of each phase. Shake and separate the solvent mixture, and place 175 ml of lower phase in each separatory funnel. Place an equal volume of upper phase in funnel 1. Make the run in the usual way, dissolving the sample in funnel 1, and transferring the upper phase to funnel 2, adding fresh upper phase to funnel 1, and so on. The materials which have high partition coefficients are then found at the end of the run in the higher numbered funnels. Here the desired product will be in tubes 5 and 6, with some left in the upper phase of 4. Separate the upper phase of 4, reextract with fresh lower phase, and combine this upper phase with both upper and lower of 5 and 6. Evaporate under reduced pressure to about $\frac{1}{4}$ volume and shake with 200 ml of EtOAc. Save this EtOAc for later use. Chill the aqueous phase, acidify with 10% citric acid to *p*H 3.5 (50 ml), and extract 3 times with 100 ml of EtOAc. Combine these EtOAc extracts with the previous EtOAc phase, wash 4 times with 200 ml of 2% citric acid, wash 3 times with H_2O, dry over $MgSO_4$, and evaporate under reduced pressure, to obtain 19.2 g of the desired product.

Commercially available *t*-butyloxycarbonyl azide (*t*-butyl azidoformate) has been widely used for the synthesis of Boc amino acids with complete success. If the reader wishes to prepare his own Boc azide, he can use the directions of Carpino (18) for synthesis of *t*-butyl carbazate, and the directions of Carpino *et al.* (19) for diazotization of the carbazate to the Boc azide.

CAUTION: Prepare and handle the Boc azide in a good hood; it is quite toxic. Inhalation of the vapor has caused severe headache and other symptoms in sensitive individuals. *Do not distill the azide;* distillation of it is unnecessary, *and has caused explosions.*

Synthesis of Boc amino acids using magnesium oxide: the Schwyzer method (116). Stir a mixture of the amino acid (20 millimoles), Boc azide (4.3 g, 30 millimoles), magnesium oxide (1.6 g, 40 millimoles), dioxane (60 ml), and water (30 ml) at 40 to 45° for 20 hours. Cool the reaction mixture, remove the magnesium oxide by filtration, and wash it twice with 100 ml of water. Extract the combined filtrate and washings 3 times with ether to remove unreacted azide. Chill the aqueous phase with ice, acidify with solid citric acid, and work up as described in the preceding section.

Synthesis of Boc amino acids in dimethyl sulfoxide (128). Although satisfactory yields of Boc derivatives of most amino acids can be obtained by one of the foregoing procedures, there are a few amino acids for which these methods fail. Since the γ-*p*-nitrobenzyl ester of glutamic acid is completely insoluble in water-containing systems, no product was obtained with the Schwyzer method. On the other hand, the dimethyl sulfoxide procedure gave a satisfactory yield. When glutamic acid γ-benzyl ester is converted to the Boc derivative in aqueous alkaline media, partial hydrolysis of the ester occurs, and the product is contaminated with Boc glutamic acid, which is very difficult to separate from the desired product. Use of such a contaminated product in peptide synthesis can lead to chain crosslinking and incorporation of γ-glutamyl residues in the peptide. The dimethyl sulfoxide procedure completely eliminated this difficulty.

Stir a mixture of 2.06 g (0.01 mole) of γ-p-nitrobenzyl glutamate, 50 ml of dimethyl sulfoxide, 2.7 ml (2.0 g, 0.02 mole) of triethyl amine (sp. gr. 0.732), and 1.5 ml (1.5 g, 0.01 mole) of Boc azide (sp. gr. 1.01) for 20 hours at room temperature. Dilute the solution with 3 volumes of water and extract 3 times with ether to remove any unreacted azide. Chill the aqueous phase, acidify with citric acid, and work up as described in the preceding sections. The product should weigh 3.8 g, and be homogeneous by TLC.

Synthesis of Boc amino acid p-nitrophenyl esters (16). Chill a solution of 4.64 g (0.02 mole) of Boc asparagine and 11.1 g (0.08 mole) p-nitrophenol in 15 ml of purified DMF (see p. 31) to 0° in an ice-salt bath, and add a solution of 4.6 g (0.022 mole) of DCC in 4 ml of DMF in portions. Let the mixture stand overnight at 4°. Remove the crystallized dicyclohexyl urea by filtration and wash with cold DMF. Evaporate the combined filtrate and washings under high vacuum from a 35° bath. Dilute the oily residue, which usually begins to crystallize, with 200 ml of absolute ether. Filter the colorless crystals and wash well with ether. The product will be pure; m. p. 163°. The large excess of p-nitrophenol promotes a high yield of the desired product, and the excess is easily removed from the product. If the Boc amino acid to be esterified is freely soluble in EtOAc, use the latter for the synthesis.

Preparation of special reagents

Preparation of 4 N HCl in dioxane. The equipment for preparing HCl-dioxane or HCl-HOAc is shown in Figure 17. Place dioxane (200 ml), purified through Al_2O_3 (see p. 31), in a 250-ml, graduated, pressure-equalizing separatory funnel. Bubble dry HCl from a cylinder through an empty safety trap into the separatory funnel by a gas inlet adapter, and attach a $CaCl_2$ drying tube to the outlet. *Watch the gas flow carefully; do* NOT *leave the operation unattended.* If HCl is passed into the dioxane nearly as fast as it can be absorbed (so that the bubbles disappear before reaching the top of the liquid), the temperature of the solution will usually rise to about 50°. When the dioxane seems to be about saturated at this temperature, close the HCl tank, clamp off the HCl inlet, and cool the HCl-dioxane to room temperature. To determine the normality of the reagents, which should be 4.0 to 4.1, dilute an aliquot of the HCl-dioxane 1:10 with water, and titrate 1 ml of this dilute acid with 0.1 N NaOH, using phenolphthalein as the indicator. If the HCl is too concentrated, add the calculated amount of dioxane to the separatory funnel to give the proper concentration. After mixing, retitrate to check that the proper dilution was made. To prevent loss of HCl on standing, the top of the reservoir must be tightly closed at all times, by removing the gas inlet tube and stoppering with a polyethylene $ stopper. The needle valve should be removed from the gas cylinder at the end of the operation, washed well with methanol, and dried thoroughly.

CAUTION: The entire operation must be done in a well-ventilated hood.

Preparation of 1 N HCl in glacial acetic acid. The procedure and setup for preparing 1 N HCl in acetic acid are the same as for preparing 4 N HCl-dioxane. Be sure to observe the precautions given there. Place reagent-grade HOAc (200 ml) from a freshly opened bottle in a pressure-equalizing separatory funnel, and bubble HCl into the acetic acid until the solution appears saturated at room temperature. Determine the concentration of HCl by the Volhard chloride-assay method (see p. 55). The HCl concentration at this stage is usually 1 to 1.1 N; higher values indicate that the HOAc is not anhydrous. Keep the separatory funnel tightly stoppered.

CAUTION: The entire operation should be done in a well-ventilated hood.

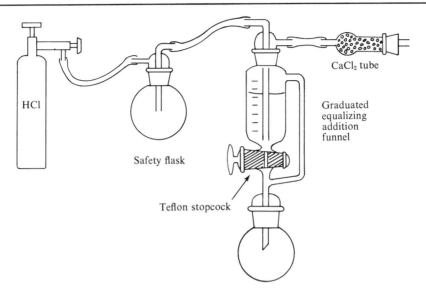

HCl

Safety flask

Teflon stopcock

CaCl₂ tube

Graduated
equalizing
addition
funnel

FIGURE 17.
Apparatus for HCl-Dioxane Preparation.

Purification of solvents

Preparation of peroxide-free dioxane. Pour dioxane through a 10 by 40 cm column of aluminum oxide (alumina, Al_2O_3). Use the column until the effluent begins to give a positive peroxide test, performed as follows: mix dioxane with an equal volume of 4% aqueous KI; the dioxane is considered peroxide-free if the solution is colorless after one minute. Purified dioxane may be stored under nitrogen in brown bottles in the cold. An alternate procedure for storing the column-purified solvent is to keep a little alumina in the bottom of the storage bottle and then filter the dioxane just before use.

CAUTION: Dioxane is reported to be toxic. Do not breathe vapors excessively.

Purification and analysis of dimethylformamide (128, 136). DMF is *very* difficult to obtain dry and free of dimethylamine. All commercial DMF, even spectroquality reagent, has been found to contain large amounts of dimethylamine.

Shake 2 liters of commercial DMF with dry KOH pellets, then decant into a round-bottom, 5,000 ml ⚷ flask with an equal volume of dry benzene (keep benzene over KOH pellets). If the KOH becomes very wet from water in the DMF, repeat the KOH drying step. Place the flask in a heating mantle, and attach a fractionating column and distilling head with appropriate condenser and adapters for collecting solvent by using an H_2O aspirator vacuum (items 8, 13, 14, Appendix B); place a drying tube and a vacuum gauge between the aspirator and the distillation apparatus. Distill the benzene without vacuum, then the DMF with vacuum. (DMF decomposes slightly when distilled at 1 atm.) Take fractions and test with dinitrofluorobenzene (FDNB) for the presence of dimethylamine as follows: mix an equal volume of FDNB solution (1 mg per ml in 95% alcohol) and DMF; let stand 30 min.; read the absorbance at 381 mμ. Blank FDNB, 0.5 mg per ml, usually reads approximately 0.2; good DMF should have a net A_{381} no higher than 0.1 to 0.15. DMF having a slightly higher absorbance can be used in the wash before and after the coupling reaction. Place the good

DMF fractions in brown bottles which should be flushed with N_2 and stored in the cold. Bottles may be sealed with rubber stopples by using a sealing device; the DMF may then be removed with a hypodermic syringe. Allow bottles to warm to room temperature before opening to avoid condensation of atmospheric water.

SOLID PHASE SYNTHESIS OF PEPTIDES

Attachment of the first amino acid to the resin

Attachment to the chloromethyl resin (72). Combine the Boc amino acid desired as the carboxyl residue in the peptide to be synthesized (1.0 mole), the chloromethyl resin (1.0 mole of Cl), and triethyl amine (0.9 mole; 0.14 ml per millimole; sp. gr. 0.723), and reflux gently in absolute EtOH for 24 to 65 hours in an oil bath heated to approximately 90°. EtOAc can be used as the refluxing solvent, and *must* be used when Boc amino acids are esterified to the nitro resin. Use enough alcohol to cover the resin (usually 2 to 5 ml per g of chloromethyl resin). Add the triethyl amine to the mixture last. Perform the reaction in a round-bottom ⚵ 24/40 flask fitted with a 500-mm H_2O condenser with a $CaCl_2$ drying tube attached. Although Merrifield stirs the reaction mixture with a magnetic stirrer, it is not essential. Most Boc amino acids are refluxed 24 hours, but Boc nitroarginine is refluxed 65 hours. The following Boc amino acids have so far been attached to the resin by this procedure: Ala, NO_2-Arg, β-Bzl-Asp, Asn, S-Bzl-Cys, γ-Bzl-Glu, Dnp-His, Gln, Gly, Ile, Leu, α-Z-Lys, ε-Z-Lys, Phe, Pro, O-Bzl-Ser, Thr, O-Bzl-Thr, Trp, O-Bzl-Tyr, Val. Acylating resin with Bzl-His and Met requires the special techniques described in the next two sections. Boc-Asn was esterified in EtOAc to avoid alcoholysis of the amide. Filter the resin in a tared, coarse-fritted Buchner funnel and wash successively with EtOH, H_2O, MeOH, and CH_2Cl_2, three times with each solvent, allowing adequate contact time for the solvent to penetrate the resin beads and for solutes to diffuse out of the beads. Transfer the resin, still suspended in CH_2Cl_2, to a separatory funnel, stir with CH_2Cl_2 (approximately 20 ml per g), and let it stand until the bulk of the resin floats to the top. Run the solvent, carrying the suspended finest particles of resin, out of the funnel and discard. Repeat this floatation three times more, each time allowing the resin to stand until a fairly sharp demarcation line appears at the bottom of the floating resin, but some particles are still suspended down in the CH_2Cl_2. Return the Boc amino acid resin which has thus been freed of fine particles to the Buchner funnel. Removal of fine resin particles in this way prevents troublesome clogging of the filter disc in the synthesis vessel. After removing all volatile solvents with a water aspirator, dry the resin overnight in a desiccator using a vacuum pump. Weigh the aminoacyl-resin, and hydrolyze about 10 mg to determine the degree of substitution of amino acid on the resin (see pp. 53–54 for details of hydrolysis and amino acid analysis methods). Yields obtained have been 0.1 to 0.5 millimoles per g of resin, using resins having 1.0 to 1.8 milliequivalents of Cl per g, which is a desirable range of substitution. Schwarz Bioresearch reports that resin with much higher substitution also gives satisfactory results. One should not try to replace all of the Cl with amino acid. As we explained on p. 7, since some Boc amino acid may be bound to quaternary amine groups on the resin by ion exchange, the values obtained on hydrolysis may be slightly higher than the actual amount esterified. For greatest accuracy, the Boc amino acid resin should be deprotected with HCl-dioxane before hydrolysis and analysis.

Attachment of Boc-im-Bzl-histidine to the hydroxymethyl resin using dicyclohexylcarbodiimide (83). Suspend hydroxymethyl resin (1.1 g, 0.49 milliequivalents of OH per g) in 10 ml of purified DMF, and add 0.54 g (1.6 millimoles) of Boc-*im*-Bzl-His. After a few minutes stirring, add 0.33 g (1.6 millimoles) of DCC; stir the mixture overnight at room temperature, with exclusion of moisture. Collect the resin in a fritted glass Buchner funnel and wash thoroughly with DMF, EtOH, and CH₂Cl₂. Dry the resin thoroughly *in vacuo* and analyze for amino acid content by hydrolysis of an aliquot (see pp. 53–54).

CAUTION: Before this aminoacyl-resin can be used for peptide synthesis involving diimide-mediated coupling steps, the remaining free hydroxyl groups on the resin must be covered by acetylation, as described below. The acetylation is not necessary if the entire procedure involves only active esters. This acetylation procedure is also useful for acetylating peptides on the resin.

Transfer the Boc-*im*-Bzl-His-resin, prepared as above, to a solid phase synthesis vessel and rock for 5 min. with 10 ml of purified DMF. Estimate the amount of free hydroxyl groups remaining on the resin from the difference between the hydroxyl content of the hydroxymethyl resin and the amount of histidine coupled to the resin. Add approximately 10 moles of acetic anhydride (mol wt 102, d 1.09) to the resin suspension for every mole of free hydroxyl groups remaining. Rock the suspension 3 min., add an amount of triethyl amine (mol wt 101, d 0.723) equivalent to the acetic anhydride, then rock the resin suspension for 2 hours. Wash the resin 3 times each with DMF, EtOH, and CH₂Cl₂. Remove fine resin particles by floatation as described in the preceding section, then transfer the resin to a fritted glass Buchner funnel, and dry *in vacuo*.

For esterification of Boc methionine to the resin, use the carbonyldiimidazole procedure described in the next section. Boc-Dnp-histidine can be coupled to the chloromethyl resin by the usual procedure, described in the preceding section.

Attachment to the hydroxymethyl resin using N,N'-carbonyldiimidazole (15). Place the Boc

amino acid desired as the carboxyl residue in the peptide to be synthesized (3 moles), the hydroxymethyl resin (1.0 mole OH), and N,N'-carbonyldiimidazole (3 moles) in purified DMF (approximately 10 ml per g of resin) in a round-bottom flask equipped with a drying tube and stir magnetically overnight. Filter the resin on a fritted glass Buchner funnel and wash thoroughly with DMF, EtOH, and CH₂Cl₂. Remove fine resin particles by floatation, then dry the resin thoroughly *in vacuo* and analyze for amino acid by hydrolysis of an aliquot (see pp. 53–54).

CAUTION: Before this aminoacyl-resin can be used for peptide synthesis involving diimide- or carbonyldiimidazole-mediated steps, the excess remaining free hydroxyl groups on the resin must be covered by acetylation; see the preceding section. If the entire synthesis will be performed by means of nitrophenyl esters, acetylation is not necessary.

Carbonyldiimidazole is quite sensitive to water, so all solvents should be carefully dried before use. This procedure, but using EtOAc as solvent, is the only one found to be satisfactory for esterification of Boc methionine to the resin (60).

Stepwise synthesis of peptides on the resin (79)

Figure 18 shows the apparatus used for the manual synthesis of peptides. (For exact descriptions of the reaction vessels and the mechanical shaker, see pp. 65–68.) The proper size for the reaction vessel is determined by the amount of resin to be used in the synthesis. The large vessel accommodates 5 to 10 g of resin; the medium vessel will handle 1.5 to 4.5 g of resin; the small vessel is used for amounts of 1 g or less. Load the Boc amino acid-resin into the reaction vessel and let it swell in dioxane for a few minutes before beginning the sequence of steps involved in building up the desired peptide. Add the solvents and reagents to the reaction vessel through the 14/20 sidearm, and

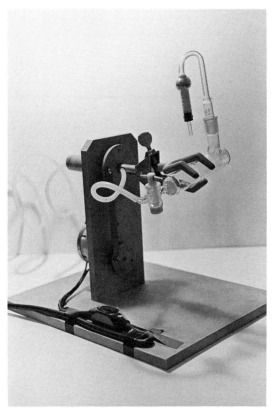

FIGURE 18.
The Shaker and Vessel Used for
Solid Phase Peptide Synthesis.

It is not always easy to carry out a long sequence of many simple, repetitive operations, such as are required in solid phase synthesis, without making a mistake. Unless an accurate, up to the minute record is kept, it is easy to become confused. We have found that the most satisfactory way to keep track of what one is doing is to fill out a data sheet as one performs each operation. (A typical data sheet for the synthesis of a pentapeptide is given on page 36.) As each operation is performed, the chart is checked and the time noted in the appropriate box.

The Boc group can also be removed with 1 N HCl-HOAc (see p. 18) instead of 4 N HCl-dioxane, but both methods have disadvantages. Whereas HOAc must be completely removed before addition of the diimide, since any trace of HOAc would cause acetylation of the amino acid on the resin instead of coupling of the desired next amino acid residue, dioxane accumulates peroxides, and so must be purified before use (see pp. 18, 31). If HCl-HOAc is used instead of HCl-dioxane, schedule A must be changed as follows: Step 1—HOAc wash, 3 times. Step 2—1 N HCl-HOAc. Step 3a—HOAc wash, 3 times. Step 3b (an additional step)—EtOH wash, 3 times. The EtOH wash is added to remove the HOAc. All traces of alcohol must be removed before addition of Et_3N, or peptide may be lost from the resin by transesterification (see p. 12).

Use purified DMF in the diimide coupling reaction instead of CH_2Cl_2 if the amino acid derivative is insoluble or only sparingly soluble in CH_2Cl_2; such derivatives are Boc-NO_2-arginine, Boc-tosyl-arginine, Boc-tryptophan, and Boc-Bzl-histidine. Dissolve the Boc amino acid in the minimum amount of DMF required, then make up the rest of the volume with CH_2Cl_2. DMF should be used only where necessary, since it is difficult to obtain free of dimethylamine, and the rearrangement of the reactive intermediate (see Fig. 15) to the unreactive acyl urea is faster in DMF than in CH_2Cl_2. If the coupling reaction is performed in DMF, the wash solvent before and after the

remove by aspiration to a large suction flask through the sintered disc at the bottom of the vessel after placing a drying tube in the side-arm. Charge the drying tube (Appendix B, item 16) with $CaCl_2$, after placing a small amount of indicator Drierite in the bulb of the tube. Keep the ⦶ stopper in the vessel at all other times, except during addition or removal of solvents.

The sequence of steps used to add each amino acid to the resin by the DCC reaction is outlined and explained in schedule A (pp. 38–39). Those who would like to follow a detailed description written in the manner of *Organic Syntheses* should refer to the directions by Merrifield and Corigliano (79) for synthesis of a tetrapeptide.

coupling step (steps 7 and 10 in schedule A) should be DMF instead of CH_2Cl_2.

The DCC-mediated coupling reaction is routine. However, if the active ester is used, such as in coupling Gln or Asn to peptide-resins, certain changes in the schedule are required. The sequence of steps used for coupling active esters is given in schedule B (p. 40). Even though it is hard to obtain DMF of adequate purity, DMF must be used instead of CH_2Cl_2 for p-nitrophenyl esters, since these amino acid derivatives do not couple in CH_2Cl_2. The larger excess of Boc amino acid active ester, the increased reaction time, and the small volume of DMF during the coupling reaction all compensate for the slower active-ester reaction.

At the end of the synthesis, remove the resin to a tared, fritted glass funnel, wash with HOAc and EtOH, and dry in a vacuum desiccator over KOH. Since some amino acid seems to be bound to the peptide-resin by ion exchange or adsorption after the coupling step, amino acid analyses of peptide-resins or of crude cleaved peptides will be more accurate if the synthesis is continued through an additional deprotection step. The HCl-dioxane (or HCl-HOAc) removes the adsorbed Boc amino acid. Take great care to wash the peptide-resin free of all excess HCl before it is stored. Record the weight of the peptide-resin. The increase in weight of the resin during the synthesis is a rough measure of the amounts of amino acids incorporated, and indicates the upper limit of the weight of peptide that might be obtained. An aliquot of the resin may be analyzed for its amino acid composition (see p. 53). The peptide is then cleaved from the resin by one of the methods described on pp. 40–46.

Peptides can very easily be synthesized at the rate of two residues a day. With efficient operation, diimide couplings can be easily carried out at the rate of three a day, especially if the third coupling reaction is allowed to continue overnight, which causes no harm. A timer may be used to turn the motor off at the end of the desired reaction time.

A TYPICAL DATA SHEET

Synthesis of: *Leu-Asp-Ala-Gly-Arg-resin*

Boc-nitroarginine-resin (0.5 g, 284 millimoles per g of resin. Total amino acid, 0.142 millimoles) was placed in the *small* reaction vessel and rocked for 5 min. in 10 ml dioxane. Used 2.5 moles of Boc amino acid and DCC per mole of *Arg*-resin. DCC reagent: 50% in CH₂Cl₂, wt/vol (1 g DCC made up to 2 ml).

Calculations:

mg Boc amino acid used

= (mmoles *Arg*-resin) × (molar excess) × (mol wt of Boc AA)

= (0.142 mmoles) × (2.5) × (mol wt of Boc AA in mg/mmole)

= (0.362) × (mol wt of Boc amino acid in mg).

ml DCC reagent

= (mmoles *Arg*-resin) × (molar excess) × (mol wt of DCC) × (solution factor)

= (0.142 mmoles) × (2.5) × (206 mg/mmole) × (2 ml/1000 mg)

= 0.15 ml.

AA	Reagent	Dioxane wash, 3 times	4 N HCl-dioxane	Dioxane wash, 3 times	CHCl₃ wash, 3 times	Et₃N:CHCl₃ (1:9)	CHCl₃ wash, 3 times	CH₂Cl₂ wash, 3 times	*Boc-AA in CH₂Cl₂	DCC	CH₂Cl₂ wash, 3 times	*mg of Boc amino acid
	Vol.	10 ml each	10 ml	10 ml each	10 ml each	10 ml (1 + 9)	10 ml each	10 ml each	6 ml	0.15 ml	10 ml each	
	Time / Date		30 min.			10 min.			5 min.	2 hours		
Gly	5-24-66	√√√	11:05-11:35	√√√	√√√	11:45-11:55	√√√	√√	12:05-12:10	12:15-2:15	√√√	0.362 × 175 = 63.4 mg
Ala	5-24-66	√√√	2:38-3:08	√√√	√√√	3:40-3:50	√√√	√√√	3:55-4:00	4:00-6:00	5-25-66 √√√	0.362 × 189 = 68.5 mg
Bzl-Asp	5-25-66	√√√	10:35-11:05	√√√	√√√	11:15-11:25	√√√	√√	11:45-11:50	11:50-2:30	√√√	Bzl-Asp 0.362 × 323 = 117 mg
Leu	5-25-66	√√√	3:05-3:35	√√√	√√√	4:40-4:50	√√√	√√√	4:55-5:00	5:00-7:00	5-26-66 √√	0.362 × 231 = 83.6 mg

Peptide-resin washed in HOAc and EtOH, and dried. Wt = 0.63 g.

Schedule A for solid phase peptide synthesis (diimide coupling)

Step	Reagent	Vol (ml)	Time (min.)
1.	Dioxane wash (3 times)	10	5
2.	4 N HCl-dioxane	10	30
3.	Dioxane wash (3 times)	10	5
4.	Chloroform wash (3 times)	10	5
5.	Et_3N-chloroform	10	10
6.	Chloroform wash (3 times)	10	5
7.	CH_2Cl_2 wash (3 times)	10	5
8.	Boc-AA in CH_2Cl_2	7	5
9.	Diimide in CH_2Cl_2	–	120
10.	CH_2Cl_2 wash (3 times)	10	5
		Total	195

INSTRUCTIONS FOR SCHEDULE A

For most rapid operation, in steps 1, 3, 4, 6, 7, and 10 shake the vessel manually between each of the three solvent washes until the resin is evenly suspended. Five minutes is usually sufficient for the three washes in this case. Add the wash solvents so that the entire inner wall of the vessel is rinsed each time, by adding part of the wash solvent so that it flows over the inner wall of the vessel with the vessel tipped slightly to one side of the horizontal, and the remainder with the vessel tipped in the other direction. Rock steps 2, 5, 8, and 9 mechanically on the peptide shaker. *All* the resin must be thoroughly washed down from the vessel walls and equilibrated with each solvent and reagent.

The wash volume is adjusted proportionally to the amount of resin used. The 10 ml wash volume is used for the small reaction vessel, designed for 1 g of resin. The wash volume for the large reaction vessel, designed for 7 to 10 g of resin, is 30 to 60 ml.

STEP 1. *Dioxane wash (3 times).*

STEP 2. *4* N *HCl-dioxane.* (See p. 30 for its preparation.)

Some CO_2 is liberated during this deprotection step. For large batches of resin, vent the vessel and retighten the stopper after most of the CO_2 has been evolved.

If Nps amino acids are used, make the following changes: In step 1, use chloroform as the wash solvent. In step 2, the reagent for deprotection is chloroform plus enough 1 N HCl in HOAc so that 3 equiv. of HCl are added to the vessel for each equiv. of Nps groups present. The time of deprotection is 10 min. In step 3, wash the peptide-resin 3 times each with chloroform, DMF, and EtOH (88). If tryptophan is present in the peptide, Nps groups must not be removed by HCl. See p. 49 for details of the thioacetamide procedure (45, 60), which is suitable.

Removal of Boc groups from some amino acids with HCl-dioxane requires full 4 N strength reagent for the 30-minute treatment time. Since the reagent is diluted somewhat by the solvent already in the resin, the deprotection conditions may be marginal. Some workers now use a prewash with HCl-dioxane (one-minute shaking), followed by the usual 30-minute treatment. This is especially important with automatic instruments, where there is additional dilution of the reagent by solvent in the connecting tubing.

STEP 3. *Dioxane wash (3 times).*

STEP 4. *Chloroform wash (3 times).*

Peptide-resin may be removed after this step for use in another peptide synthesis or for analysis. Sometimes an EtOH wash is added after the dioxane wash and before resin is removed, since $CHCl_3$ suspensions of resin may be difficult to handle. After a final deprotection (see p. 7), wash the resin at least 6 times with EtOH.

STEP 5. *Et_3N-chloroform.*

The reagent is prepared by adding 1 vol of reagent grade triethyl amine to 9 vol of reagent chloroform. Mix the reagent just before adding it.

STEP. 6. *Chloroform wash (3 times).*

STEP 7. *CH_2Cl_2 wash (3 times).*

STEP 8. *Boc-AA in CH_2Cl_2.*

The number of moles of Boc amino acid is usually 2.5 times the number of moles of the first amino acid on the resin. Larger excesses of Boc amino acid and DCC have been used where steric hindrance has caused lower yields in the coupling reaction. The volume of solvent should be kept low during the coupling step to promote the coupling reaction and minimize the rearrangement to the acyl urea by-product.

STEP 9. *Diimide in CH_2Cl_2.*

The quantity of DCC (1 g made up to 2 ml with CH_2Cl_2) used is equimolar to the Boc amino acid added at step 8. If the DCC contains some dicyclohexyl urea (precipitate in the CH_2Cl_2 solution), the amount may be increased slightly. Prolongation of the coupling reaction beyond 2 hours is of questionable advantage, since the active intermediate may have all rearranged to acyl urea in this time. If there is evidence of poor coupling, it may be more profitable to repeat the coupling reaction with fresh quantities of Boc amino acid and DCC. Before doing so, one may find it advantageous to wash the peptide-resin 3 times with HOAc to remove precipitated acyl urea, then wash it with EtOH, then proceed with step 4.

WARNING: DCC may cause severe allergic reactions in sensitive persons. Avoid all contact with the skin or mucosa. Wash immediately with acetone after any contact. In order to prevent DCC contamination of the balances, transfer the DCC in the hood over disposable paper into a tared vial. Reweigh the vial with DCC in it, and add 1 ml CH_2Cl_2 for every g of DCC; this gives a 50% DCC solution. Prepare enough DCC reagent for the entire synthesis. *Do not pipette the DCC solution by mouth.*

STEP 10. *CH_2Cl_2 wash (3 times).*

When left overnight, the peptide-resin is left at this stage, suspended in CH_2Cl_2.

Schedule B for solid phase peptide synthesis (active ester coupling)

Step	Reagent	Time (min.)
1.	Dioxane wash (3 times)	5
2.	4 *N* HCl-dioxane	30
3.	Dioxane wash (3 times)	5
4.	Chloroform wash (3 times)	5
5.	Et₃N-chloroform	10
6.	Chloroform wash (3 times)	5
7.	DMF wash (3 times)	5
8.	Boc-AA active ester in DMF	240
9.	DMF wash (3 times)	5
	Total	310

INSTRUCTIONS FOR SCHEDULE B

STEPS 1 TO 6.

Since steps 1 to 6 are the same in schedules A and B, the general instructions and the instructions for these steps are the same for both schedules.

STEP 7. *DMF wash (3 times).*

Use DMF of the highest obtainable purity in the last wash before adding the Boc amino acid active ester and in the coupling reaction. DMF of lesser purity may be used in the other DMF washes.

STEP 8. *Boc-AA active ester in DMF.*

Use the minimum volume of DMF required to suspend the resin. Use 4 moles of Boc amino acid active ester per mole of the first amino acid on the resin. Greater excesses of active esters and longer coupling times have been used where the coupling reaction was slow. To recover the unreacted excess Boc amino acid active ester from the reaction filtrate, dilute the DMF with water, extract the ester into CHCl₃ or EtOAc, and repurify the recovered material by an appropriate method.

STEP 9. *DMF wash (3 times).*

When left overnight, the peptide-resin is given 3 CH₂Cl₂ washes and left in CH₂Cl₂.

Cleavage of the peptide from the resin

Cleavage by HBr-TFA. The apparatus for cleavage of the peptide from the resin using HBr-TFA is shown in Figure 19. Suspend the peptide-resin in trifluoroacetic acid (10 ml per g of resin) in the cleavage vessel. If the peptide contains cysteine, methionine, or tyrosine, in addition to benzyl or carbobenzoxy groups, dissolve 50 moles of anisole or methyl ethyl sulfide in the TFA for each mole of sensitive amino acid (see pp. 9, 21); 15 moles of methionine per mole of sensitive residues has also been found to give satisfactory protection (80). Bubble a slow stream of anhydrous HBr for 90 min. into the suspension by means of a bleeder tube and out through a drying tube containing CaCl₂. A shorter cleavage time may be desired (see p. 11). If the peptide contains tyrosine or tryptophan, bubble the HBr through a scrubber tube containing a solution of 2 g of anisole or resorcinol in TFA. Use a trap between the HBr cylinder and the cleavage vessel. The HBr flow must be adjusted occasionally, since the needle valve often tends to shut itself off, and if it does, the solvent will be sucked back into the tubing. After 90 min., close the HBr tank and clamp off the HBr inlet. Open the stopcock at the base of the cleavage vessel, and aspirate the peptide in the HBr-TFA into an appropriate round-bottom flask. The suction may be applied by means of a water pump. Use a CaCl$_2$ drying tube in the aspirator line to prevent moisture from being sucked back into the flask. Remove the HBr valve after each use, wash with methanol, and dry thoroughly.

Wash the resin 3 times with TFA (10 ml per g of resin each time), allowing the TFA to extract the resin about a minute with each wash, then evaporate the peptide solution to dryness under reduced pressure without heating. Dissolve the peptide several times in a suitable solvent, HOAc–H$_2$O (3:1) or MeOH–H$_2$O (1:1), and evaporate the solvent under reduced pressure to remove excess HBr (the peptide is always quite acidic at this stage). If the cleavage solution contained anisole, extract the crude product thoroughly with ether (Sephadex chromatography has also been used for removal of anisole, methionine, and ethyl methyl sulfide),

then dry the peptide under high vacuum. The crude peptide from HBr-TFA cleavage always contains much nonpeptide material, so the weight at this point is not a true index of the yield. Yields of crude peptide can be based on amino acid analysis of hydrolysates.

CAUTION: The entire cleavage process should be done in a good hood. Trifluoroacetic acid causes serious burns; give any spillage on the skin immediate attention. *Do not breathe the TFA vapor.*

The use of anhydrous HF in solid phase synthesis (by A. B. Robinson).   HF is very easily handled in a Teflon–Kel-F line. However, it can cause severe burns and is quite poisonous. No operation should be performed which can possibly lead to contact with the liquid or vapors. Keep available in the laboratory a 20% solution of calcium gluconate in glycerin.

The commonest HF burns result from accidental contact with HF after which the HF is not completely washed from under the fingernails, and, several hours later, causes a painful burn. The pain can be alleviated by applying calcium gluconate. After contact with HF, wash

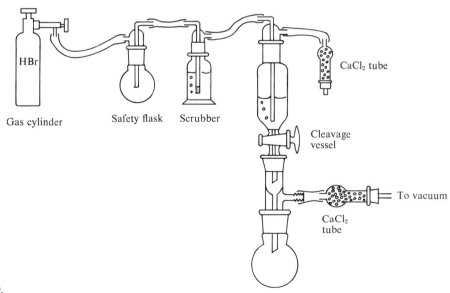

FIGURE 19.
Cleavage of Peptides with HBr-TFA.

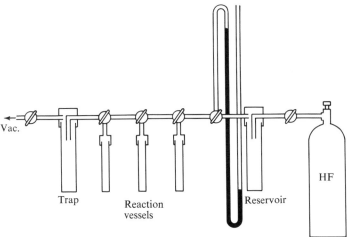

FIGURE 20.
Diagram of HF Apparatus.

liberally with water and soak in water, then apply calcium gluconate.

The entire HF operation *must* be carried out in a good hood: *breathing HF causes death.*

CONSTRUCTION OF AN HF LINE. Figures 20 and 21 show HF lines quite adequate for these reactions (52, 101, 106). The primary requirements for the line are:

1. The materials used must be inert to HF. Teflon and Kel-F are used in the illustrated lines. No metal should come in contact with the HF gas or liquid.

2. The line must be vacuum-tight and also pressure-tight to at least two atmospheres internal pressure.

3. The volumes of HF must be easily measurable. The vessels in the illustrated lines are Kel-F, which is translucent.

The line diagrammed in Figure 20 is commercially available (see Appendix B, item 32).

The line illustrated in Fig. 21 can be constructed in two days with an expenditure of $250 for materials. The valves and connectors are commercially available Teflon pieces, and the rest of the line is machined from Kel-F rod. The flange clamp fittings used in the line-vessel connections are convenient. Viton rubber O-rings are used to seal these connections, and should be changed periodically. (See Appendix B, items 33 and 34.)

A workable HF line has also been assembled from polyethylene tubing and stopcocks and polypropylene tees and screw-cap bottles (97; see Appendix B, items 35, 44, 48, and 49). The tubing was cold-shrunk into undersized holes in the bottle caps, and Teflon tape was used for sealing threads. The total cost of such apparatus would be very much less than for either of those described above, but users should be warned to be especially careful of leaks or vacuum collapse. Dangers arise both from possible admission of water vapor into the system and from HF burns and poisoning. Those who designed this line use a stream of dry N_2, rather than vacuum, to remove HF.

USING THE HF LINE. Any refrigerant of a temperature low enough to condense HF is suitable for its distillation. Liquid nitrogen is the easiest to use, but CO_2-acetone is satisfactory. Although an aspirator will suffice, it is preferable to use a vacuum pump isolated from the line by a liquid nitrogen-cooled trap and a KOH trap. For most convenient operation, use both a vacuum pump and a water aspirator, each connected to the HF line by a 3-way stopcock. Although these reactions seem to proceed satisfactorily with no special precautions about H_2O, it is preferable to dry the HF over CoF_3 in the reservoir vessel. Both the reservoir vessel and the reaction vessel should have Teflon-covered magnetic stirring bars to avoid bumping and to permit distillation at a reasonable rate. The volume of HF used is measured by calibrating the reservoir vessel and observing the amount distilled from it.

A typical experiment is as follows.

1. Place a stirring bar and a few grams of CoF_3 in the reservoir vessel.

2. Place the dry peptide-resin and a stirring bar in the reaction vessel. Add at least 50 equivalents of anisole per equivalent of peptide if sensitive amino acids are present along with carbobenzoxy, benzyl, or nitro protecting groups.

3. Fill the reservoir and trap Dewars with liquid nitrogen and wait for a few minutes. Kel-F has a low thermal conductivity, and the inside of the vessels will require a few minutes to become safely cold.

4. Open the vacuum-pump valve and evacuate the line. Do not pump long enough to distill the anisole.

5. Close all valves.

6. Slowly open the HF tank valve and distill HF into the reservoir vessel. It is convenient to store enough HF for several reactions in the reservoir.

7. Turn off the HF tank valve and let the reservoir vessel warm to room temperature. A stirred beaker of water will speed heat transfer. Magnetic stirring bars in the plastic vessel and in the water beaker can be stirred simultaneously with the same stirring motor. Continue stirring at a rate which keeps the CoF_3 freely suspended in the liquid HF.

8. Now cool the reaction vessel and slowly open the valve between the reservoir vessel and the reaction vessel so that the HF in the reservoir vessel boils gently. In the presence of anhydrous HF, peptide-resins turn a deep blue. In the presence of anisole and HF, they turn red. When the desired amount of HF has distilled, close all valves and place a stirred bath

FIGURE 21.
Photograph of HF Apparatus.

of the desired temperature around the reaction vessel. Stir the reaction mixture for the desired length of time.

9. When the reaction is complete, continue stirring and *cautiously* open the valve between the reaction vessel and the trap. Distill all HF into the trap vessel.

10. Throughout steps 6 to 9, the vacuum pump has been isolated from the line. The system should still be under the pressure only of HF. After all the HF has distilled from the reaction vessel, open the line to the pump to effect complete removal of the anisole and the red-orange material. This may take an hour.

11. When the sample is dry, suspend the resin in dry EtOAc and transfer to a peptide cleavage vessel (see Fig. 25). Several washes with EtOAc will remove the last traces of anisole and its oxidation products. Dry the resin *in vacuo* and extract the peptide with a suitable solvent.

a. With peptides of low molecular weight, dissolve the sample in a few ml of 1% HOAc, filter off the resin, and immediately freeze-dry.

b. With large peptides and proteins, immediate desalting on a Sephadex column is preferable. Pyridine or HOAc is useful for extracting water-insoluble peptides from the resin.

12. HF can be most conveniently disposed of by pumping it from the trap vessel directly into the aspirator.

The vessels may be conveniently washed with soap and water, then rinsed with distilled water. Occasionally, the line may be disassembled and boiled in HNO_3. It is very important to keep the HF apparatus *free* of metals, especially with proteins, peptides containing charged side chains, and porphyrins. With proteins, the HF must be dried over CoF_3.

CHEMISTRY. Though we have rationalized mechanisms to direct our experiments, the real mechanisms of the HF reactions here are virtually unknown. Some facts may, however, be helpful.

1. We have used HF on solid phase peptide-resins containing all the common amino acids

with good results (101). A typical procedure is 100 micromoles peptide-resin, 0.5 ml anisole (5 millimoles), and 5.0 ml HF, reacted at 0° for 30 min.

2. N–O acyl migration does not appear to be a serious problem. In any case, it can be reversed easily by weak base.

3. The only amino acid which has not, at present, been successfully blocked for Merrifield synthesis and unblocked by HF is histidine. However, see p. 20.

4. Several proteins remain biologically active after long exposure to HF. Cytochromes, however, and other heme proteins lose their Fe completely on contact with HF. If the HF is dry and metal-free, the cytochrome, too, can be returned to biological activity by reinsertion of the Fe. Nonheme iron proteins are similarly bleached.

5. Cysteine peptides are in the free SH form after the freeze-drying, and can be used for further reactions immediately (see p. 48).

6. If O-benzyl tyrosine is present, the reaction time should be at least 1 hour at 0°.

Cleavage by ammonia (14, 128). Saturate anhydrous methanol with anhydrous ammonia at 0°. Add the peptide-resin (10 ml solvent per g of resin) and a magnetic stirring bar, wire or tape a tight stopper in place, and stir the suspension at room temperature for 2 days. Open the vessel, remove the resin by filtration, wash it with methanol, and evaporate the combined filtrate and washings *in vacuo*. For peptides not soluble in methanol, use an appropriate solvent.

CAUTION: The entire operation must be conducted in a good hood.

Somewhat higher yields of some peptides have been obtained by suspending the peptide-resin in purified dioxane, chilling the suspension, adding an equal volume of cold, ammonia-saturated methanol, stoppering, and stirring as above (128). Mixtures of ammonia-saturated methanol and DMF have also been used (44). If ammonolysis of peptides from the resin is unsatisfactory the peptide may be first removed from the resin as the methyl ester by transesterification, then converted to the amide in solution.

Cleavage by hydrazine (93). Suspend the peptide-resin in purified DMF (5 ml per g of resin) and add anhydrous hydrazine (30 equiv. per equiv. of peptide). Stir the mixture for 2 days at room temperature. Remove the resin by filtration and wash with DMF. Evaporate the combined filtrate and washings *in vacuo*, and purify the peptide hydrazide by a suitable procedure.

Since Boc and formyl amine protecting groups and *t*-butyl esters remain intact during the hydrazinolysis, they can be used to produce protected peptide hydrazides suitable for further coupling in solution. Methyl and benzyl esters on side chains will be converted to hydrazides.

The procedure of Honda *et al.* (37) may be used to prepare anhydrous hydrazine from the hydrate. Add one kg of hydrazine hydrate during 3 hours from a dropping funnel to a gently refluxing mixture of 2 liters toluene and 2 kg CaO. Continue refluxing for 10 hours, then distill the anhydrous hydrazine into a Dean-Stark receiver (see Appendix B, item 24). Remove the hydrazine, which collects as the lower layer, and return the toluene to the flask. The yield, which is about 75%, can be improved on successive runs by reusing the same toluene.

Cleavage by transesterification (56).

METHYL ESTERS. Suspend the peptide-resin in anhydrous methanol (40 ml per g of resin), and add triethyl amine (50 moles per mole of peptide). Stir the mixture at room temperature for 20 hours. Remove the resin by filtration, evaporate the solvent, and purify the peptide ester by a suitable technique.

ETHYL ESTERS. Stir a suspension of peptide-resin in 10% Et$_3$N–EtOH at 45° for 90 hours. A fair yield of peptide benzyl ester has been similarly obtained by reaction at 80° for 40 hours. Other primary alcohols have been simi-larly used. B. Halpern has found that transesterification is inhibited in rigorously dried reagents.

Deprotection of finished peptides

Hydrogenation under pressure. The hydrogenation is carried out using a Parr low-pressure, shaker-type hydrogenation apparatus. This procedure includes details for monitoring the reduction of nitroarginine to arginine, but aliquots may also be removed to test for the hydrogenolysis of other protecting groups.

Dissolve the sample to be hydrogenated in MeOH-HOAc-H$_2$O (10:1:1), usually about 10 to 20 mg per ml, and place in the hydrogenator bottle. Add the catalyst, 5% Pd on BaSO$_4$ (51). For hydrogenolysis of nitroarginine, a weight of catalyst equal to the weight of crude peptide will usually give complete reaction overnight. For hydrogenolysis of benzyl histidine, more catalyst and a longer time may be necessary. Take an 0.1 ml sample for analysis; save for comparison with the aliquot taken after hydrogenation.

INSTRUCTIONS FOR OPERATING THE H$_2$ TANK. Open the main valve of the H$_2$ tank. Open the valve to the reservoir of the hydrogenator. With the cylinder needle valve, add H$_2$ to the reservoir to between 50 and 55 lbs. Close the cylinder needle valve. Close the main H$_2$ valve, and release pressure in the cylinder needle valve by opening it. Reclose the reservoir valve and the cylinder needle valve.

Place the bottle, with the protector shield on it, in position and evacuate the bottle with a water aspirator. The solvent bubbles at first and then ceases to bubble. Close the valve to the aspirator and fill the bottle with H$_2$ by opening the valve from the reservoir to the bottle. Close the valve from the reservoir to the bottle, and repeat the evacuation and filling process twice. Leave the valve between the H$_2$ reservoir and the bottle open during the reduction. Shake overnight. Close the valve to the reservoir and bleed the H$_2$ from the bottle before loosening the bottle clamp. Remove an 0.1 ml aliquot to test the completeness of hydrogenolysis, as follows. Add 1 ml MeOH and 9 ml H_2O to the aliquots taken before and after the reduction. For nitroarginine the process of the hydrogenolysis is monitored by observing the disappearance of the ultraviolet absorption at 271 mμ due to nitroarginine ($\epsilon = 14,970$) and the appearance of a positive Sakaguchi reaction (see p. 56) due to the free guanidine group of arginine. For histidine peptides, removal of the benzyl group from the imidazole nucleus is monitored by appearance of a positive Pauly reaction (see p. 56). Electrophoresis or chromatography are also helpful for determining completeness of hydrogenolysis. After the reduction is complete, filter the reduced peptide through a washed $\frac{1}{4}$-inch celite pad and evaporate under reduced pressure (flash evaporator). Dry in a desiccator *in vacuo* over KOH. The peptide is now ready to be purified.

The palladium in the recommended catalyst is present as the brown oxide; it is reduced to the black metal at the beginning of the shaking. Strong acids (HCl) cannot be used, since the PdO will dissolve. Palladium on carbon catalyst can also be used, but is less active. If it is used, the catalyst must be wet first with the water, since the dry catalyst will ignite methanol and other flammable solvents. All hydrogenation catalysts are pyrophoric after the hydrogenation; do not suck air through them on the filter for any extended time.

Hydrogenation at atmospheric pressure. Dissolve the crude peptide either in MeOH with 10% HOAc and 10% H_2O or in 90% HOAc in H_2O in a $\mathring{S}$ round-bottom flask. Add the catalyst, 5% Pd on $BaSO_4$ (about 1.5 times the weight of peptide), to the flask containing the dissolved peptide. Remove a sample for analysis as described in the preceding section. The apparatus for hydrogenation is shown in Figure 22. Fill the gas-washing bottle with water to prevent excessive evaporation of solvent during the hydrogenation, and allow the operator to estimate the rate of gas flow. Bubble N_2

through the reaction mixture for 10 min. then very slowly bubble H_2 through it for 15 hours at room temperature. Vent the H_2 outlet into the hood flue. Stir the reaction mixture magnetically throughout the operation. Flush N_2 through the line for about 10 min. before opening the vessel. Analyze, filter, and evaporate the reduced peptide to dryness as in the preceding section.

Deprotection by sodium and liquid ammonia. The apparatus shown in Figure 23 is suitable for removing S-benzyl, *im*-benzyl, and guanidino-tosyl groups from simple peptides. The ball joint connecting the two flasks provides flexibility. The ammonia inlet tube should extend nearly to the bottom of the drying flask. Fill the drying tubes with KOH pellets. Assemble the entire apparatus with glass-covered stirring bars in the flasks and silicone grease on the joints. Place the protected peptide in the reaction flask, and pump the entire apparatus overnight on high vacuum, then allow air to enter slowly through the drying tube.

No more than 100 mg of peptide should be reduced at one time; this will require at least 100 ml of ammonia in the reaction vessel. Add a small piece of sodium (freshly cut under dry toluene) to the drying flask. Cool the drying flask in a bath of ethanol and solid CO_2, and condense enough ammonia for the peptide at hand from the cylinder into the drying flask. Excess sodium, as indicated by the blue color, must be present throughout the subsequent distillation of ammonia into the reaction flask.

Transfer the freezing bath to the reaction flask, and distill the ammonia over. Smooth distillation may be aided by stirring. The ammonia in the reaction flask should not be high enough to cover the ammonia inlet tube. When enough ammonia has been condensed in the reaction flask, remove the freezing bath, start the stirrer, and add *small* pieces of sodium, freshly cut under dry toluene and transferred without blotting to the flask with the aid of polyethylene-tipped forceps. All traces of iron must be avoided, since it catalyzes the conver-

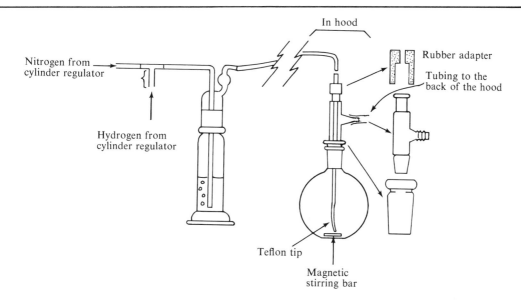

FIGURE 22.
Hydrogenation at Atmospheric Pressure.

sion of Na in NH_3 to $NaNH_2$. Vapors of CO_2 from the bath must not touch the sodium or enter the flask. If the ammonia is boiling during the addition of sodium, the escaping vapors help prevent the entrance of water vapor. Let each piece of sodium dissolve completely be- fore adding another. As the end of the reaction is approached, the pieces of sodium should be very small, so that a large excess of sodium is never present. The end-point is indicated by a stable, very light-blue color in the peptide- ammonia solution. When the blue color has

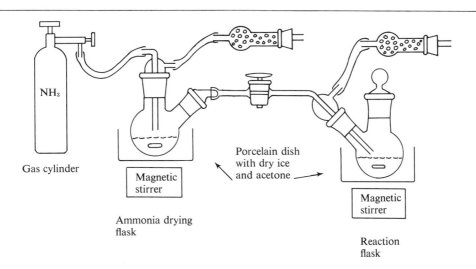

FIGURE 23.
Apparatus for Na–NH_3 Reduction.

been maintained for the desired length of time (see third paragraph below), quench the reaction by adding enough dry ammonium chloride to react with the sodium added (equivalent to the sum of carboxyl, hydroxyl, and deprotected groups).

Let the ammonia evaporate, with stirring (vent into the hood flue). Remove the last traces of ammonia by pumping the flask (through the drying tube) first on the water aspirator, then on a well-trapped vacuum pump. Dissolve the peptide residue in dilute acetic acid or HCl, being careful that the solution does not remain basic any longer than necessary. There is *a danger of explosion* if $NaNH_2$ or unreacted Na is present.

Cysteine-containing peptides can be stabilized for purification in the reduced state by conversion to the S-sulfonate (3, 23). Alternatively, they can be oxidized to the disulfide at pH 6.8 by ferricyanide (38), or by iron-catalyzed air oxidation (137).

Much discussion has centered on how long a stable blue end-point should be maintained before quenching the reduction. Early workers used extremely long times (15 to 30 min.). However, recent work with longer peptides has shown that many peptides are seriously degraded by the $Na-NH_3$ reaction. Thr-Pro and Arg-Pro bonds are especially labile (8, 98). Marglin and Merrifield (62) found that satisfactory yields of the insulin B-chain could be obtained only if the stable blue color was quenched after 15 seconds, and then only if a large excess of sodium was never present. To improve the reduction, Merrifield (77) designed a chilled addition funnel, in which sodium was dissolved in liquid ammonia. This ammonia solution was then added to the reaction vessel in such a way that no large excess was ever present. A similar approach has been used by Bayer *et al.* (5, 6). It is much more difficult to control the amount of excess sodium present when the metal is added directly to the reaction flask. An apparatus for preparing and using $Na-NH_3$ solutions has been described (89).

Recent evidence indicates that not all peptides can be satisfactorily deblocked by $Na-NH_3$. A 45-residue peptide which contained two Bzl-His residues and four Pro residues, two in the Thr-Pro linkages, never gave a satisfactory endpoint (94). Proline began to degrade before removal of benzyl groups from histidine was complete.

CAUTION: The entire operation must be done in a good hood in a room where ninhydrin reactions are not done. *Metallic sodium* is extremely caustic and *explodes on contact with water.* Ammonia is very caustic to the eyes, and appropriate first aid should be readily available.

Specific techniques
with tryptophan residues

Because of the well-known acid lability of tryptophan, the synthesis of tryptophan-containing peptides by the solid phase method has been approached with some hesitancy. However, it appears that, with minor modifications of the standard procedure, tryptophan can be handled satisfactorily in SPPS. The two points in the synthetic procedure which offer a potential hazard are the deprotection of Boc groups and the cleavage of the finished peptide from the resin.

Two apparently satisfactory methods for removing Boc groups from tryptophan-containing peptide-resins are available. M. E. Lombardo and R. Piasio at Schwarz Bioresearch (56) have found that the HCl-HOAc reagent can be used without damage to tryptophan if the temperature is lowered to near the freezing point of the solvent. For this purpose they constructed a jacketed reaction vessel and circulated water at 15° through the jacket during the deprotection and acid-wash steps. At this temperature, deprotection was prolonged to 45 min., and no significant oxidation of tryptophan occurred during the synthesis. In a different approach, G. R. Marshall, at Washington University (64), has incorporated a reducing agent into the acidic media. To the standard HCl-HOAc reagent he added 1% 2-mercaptoethanol, then used this modified reagent at room temperature. He also added mercapto-ethanol to the HOAc washes after the HCl-HOAc step. Use of mercaptoethanol will cause difficulty if a subsequent hydrogenation step is used. In any event, hydrogenation may be hazardous for tryptophan peptides. Removal of Boc groups with TFA appeared to be less satisfactory.

A logical development of this approach would be the addition of mercaptoethanol to the HCl-dioxane reagent. The thiol should both prevent peroxide formation in the reagent and protect the tryptophan, making the advantages of the dioxane reagent available for use with trypto-phan peptides.*

When the Nps protecting group is used in the synthesis of tryptophan-containing peptides, HCl cannot be used for deprotection. The following procedure has been found satisfactory for SPPS (45, 60), and is to be substituted for steps 1, 2, and 3 of schedule A: Step 1—HOAc wash (3 times). Step 2—suspend the resin in MeOH–HOAc (4:1 by volume, 5 ml per g of resin), add thioacetamide (20 moles per mole of Nps groups), and rock for 30 min. Step 3—wash resin with MeOH and HOAc (3 times each).

Anhydrous HF can be used to cleave trypto-phan-containing peptides from the resin with-out loss of any tryptophan (64). This was to be expected, since Sakakibara had already shown that HF does not damage tryptophan (106). Cleavage with HBr-TFA caused at least a 15% loss of tryptophan. As alternate methods of cleavage, any of the basic reagents can be used. Ammonolysis (64), transesterification with an alcohol and triethyl amine (56), and sodium ethoxide cleavage (55) have all been used sucess-fully for tryptophan-containing peptides.

The amino acid analysis of tryptophan in peptides presents a special problem, since the usual acid hydrolysis cannot be used. The usual approach to this problem has been to use alkaline hydrolysis (86, 99). Hydrolyze peptides in sealed, evacuated Pyrex tubes with 12% NaOH for 22 hours at 110°. Acidify the hy-drolyzate to pH 2 with HCl, and remove by filtration the silicic acid resulting from attack on the glass by alkali. Dilute the sample to a sodium concentration of no greater than 0.2 M before applying it to the amino acid analyzer. An approach which avoids the formation of silicic acid uses screw-capped Teflon tubes, and hydrolysis with 15% NaOH for 16 hours at 110° (90), although it is sometimes hard to get a good seal. Marshall (64) found that the most reliable and consistent results with tryptophan peptides could be obtained by complete enzymatic hy-drolysis of them. A new method for rapid enzymatic total hydrolysis has been developed by Keutmann and Potts (46; see p. 54). Their method uses successive treatments with large amounts of papain and aminopeptidase M, and appears to be free of the difficulties encountered with leucineaminopeptidase, which failed to cleave Arg-Pro and Asp-X bonds. A spectro-photometric method for measuring tryptophan based on loss of UV absorption after treatment with N-bromosuccinimide has been described (125).

TECHNIQUES FOR PURIFICATION OF PEPTIDES

Purification by countercurrent distribution

Countercurrent distribution has been used to purify many peptides synthesized by solid phase. Although long CCD runs are required for very high resolution, most peptides prepared by the solid phase method, especially ones of moderate size, are fairly pure as cleaved from the resin, and short CCD runs will provide the necessary purification. Runs of 100 to 300 transfers are usually adequate. CCD has the advantages that fairly large amounts of material can be handled with much greater ease than they can be with

---

*E. Kaiser and R. Colescott have recently used such a reagent successfully for the synthesis of tryptophan pep-tides.

column chromatography, and that purification by CCD usually takes less time. (For details of the procedure, see 20, 21, 34.)

A particular problem with CCD that must be kept in mind is selection of a solvent system which will provide a satisfactory k without causing degradation of the peptide or intractable emulsification, and from which the product can be recovered without too much difficulty. Salt-containing systems, which have been so useful for proteins, cause difficulty with small peptides, since dialysis cannot be used to separate the peptide from the salt. In general, where buffering is desired, volatile systems using ammonia or pyridine with acetic or formic acid have proved most satisfactory. Moderate amounts of salts may be removed by gel filtration on Sephadex columns, but inconveniently large columns are required if the salt concentration is high.

After completion of the CCD run, peptide peaks are located by applying a quantitative reagent (see pp. 55–57; see also the section after this one).

Purity of peptides can be demonstrated by analysis of aliquots from both upper and lower phases of each tube across the peak; the k will be constant across the peak if the substance is pure. The shape of the peak should also conform to the theoretical curve. For more rapid location of peaks when purity is to be established by some other criteria, one need sample only the lower phase of the first half of the train and the upper phase of the second half.

Aliquots for analysis should be as small as is compatible with accurate analysis, since large samples of upper phase may not be miscible with the analytical reagents. In butanol systems, aliquots of 0.05 to 0.2 ml are usually satisfactory, whereas larger ones will have to be evaporated.

The following are some systems which have been found useful (solvent ratios are by volume):
1-butanol, 1% trifluoroacetic acid (bradykinin, k 1.2);
1-butanol, 0.4 M ammonium acetate, pH 7 (angiotensin I, k 0.8; angiotensin II, k 0.13);

1-butanol, acetic acid, water, 4:1:5 (angiotensin II, k 0.3);
1-butanol, 2% formic acid;
1-butanol, pyridine, acetic acid, water, 150:2:0.2:150 (or 8:2:1:9);
1-butanol, benzene, TFA, water, 135:15:3:150 (bradykininyl-bradykinin, k 2);
1-butanol, pyridine, 0.1% acetic acid, 790:475:1735 (insulin A- and B-chain S-sulfonates);
0.086% trichloroacetic acid in 2-butanol, water, propionic acid, 87:110:15, the TCA being extracted from the purified material with ether (Bence-Jones protein, k 0.5);
88% phenol, ethanol, 0.1 N HCl, 1750:895:2510 (hemoglobin tryptic peptides); and
acetic acid, water, 2-butanol, cyclohexane, pyridine, 30:70:60:40:2 (tyrocidin C, k 0.8).

Column chromatography

Ion-exchange column chromatography is the most widely used technique for separating and purifying peptides because of its great versatility and extreme selectivity. Significant amounts of peptides can easily be handled in a single run (though not as much as with CCD), even though a single run sometimes takes a long time. A brief guide to some different types of chromatography is presented in this section. Ion exchangers based on cellulose have been superior for large peptides and proteins. General information is available in recent books (2, 36). Systems useful with peptides all use volatile buffers.

Chromatography on Dowex 1 (28).   Dowex 1 is a strongly basic resin composed of quaternary ammonium groups on a crosslinked polystyrene matrix. The system of Funatsu (28) allows the entire range of peptides, from strongly basic to strongly acidic, to be chromatographed in a single run on this resin. For separation of such a complete mixture, the sample is adsorbed to the acetate form of the resin at high pH (8.8, pyridine-collidine). The peptides are eluted, first with a gradient of decreasing pH pyridine-collidine-acetate buffers, and then with a gradient of increasing concentration of acetic acid. The entire system takes 3 days, but for the purification of synthetic peptides, only a short part of the entire system will generally need to be used. Basic peptides (especially those containing much arginine) are eluted first, followed by the neutral, and then the acidic peptides. Peptides containing a high percentage of aromatic amino acids will be retarded more than would be expected from their net charge.

Dowex 1 × 2 resin is converted to the acetate form by cycling batchwise with 1 N NaOH, 1 N HCl, 1 N NaOH, and 50% HOAc using H_2O washes after each cycle. A 0.9 by 150 cm column of this resin, operated at 40°, will handle up to 30 micromoles (100 mg) of a peptide mixture, somewhat less if the sample is largely one peptide. The solvent gradients are established with a Varigrad, and are pumped through the column by a metering pump. (For details of solvent preparation, see 28.)

After the end of the run (50% HOAc elution), the column can be prepared for reuse without repouring by washing it with water and then equilibrating it with the starting buffer by pumping it overnight or until the effluent reaches the proper pH.

Chromatography on Dowex 50 (112). Dowex 50 is a strongly acidic resin bearing sulfonic acid groups on a crosslinked polystyrene matrix. The procedure of Schroeder (112) allows a wide range of peptides to be separated on this resin by buffers of volatile pyridine in acetic acid. One hazard in the use of Dowex 50 is that peptides with a high proportion of aromatic amino acids may be irreversibly bound to the resin.

Dowex 50 is cycled with NaOH and HCl, and converted to the pyridine salt with 2 M pyridine. The resin is equilibrated in a pH 3.1 buffer of pyridine in acetic acid (0.2 M in pyridine), and the column is run at 38° with a gradient from the equilibrating buffer to pH 5.0, 2 M pyridine buffer, and then with a pH 5.6, 8.5 M pyridine buffer. (For details of buffer preparation and operation, see 112.)

Chromatography on IRC-50 (25, 72). IRC-50 is a weak acid resin, bearing carboxyl groups. It is especially useful with basic peptides; aromatic residues do not have any great affinity for it, and acidic peptides may not be held on columns of it. IRC-50 is cycled with acid and base, and converted to the free-acid form by washing with 50% HOAc. When cycled with acid or base, the resin does not neutralize instantaneously, as the strong acid and strong base resins do, and must be allowed to stand with the reagent for about 30 min.

Columns of IRC-50 can be run in two different ways. Peptides can be adsorbed to the hydrogen form of the column from solution in water and eluted with a gradient of increasing strength of acetic acid (72). A basic peptide, such as bradykinin, will elute from the column with approximately 35% HOAc. Higher resolving power is obtained by eluting the peptides with ammonium acetate or pyridine acetate buffers of increasing pH, or by increasing ionic strength at constant pH (25). In this type of operation, bradykinin will be eluted at approximately pH 6.8, with a 0.125 M ammonium acetate buffer.

Gel chromatography. Chromatography on dextran or polyacrylamide gels is a very useful technique for separating peptides from salt and other contaminants of low molecular weight, and for separating peptides on the basis of molecular weight. A good recent source for both general and specific information on gel chromatography is H. Determann, *Gel Chromatography* (Springer, 1968).

Analysis of effluent fractions. Peptides can be located in the eluates by the quantitative ninhydrin or Folin-Lowry reactions, or by one of the reagents for specific amino acid residues (see pp. 56–57). The Folin-Lowry method is more sensitive, especially for large peptides. Sensitivity of the ninhydrin reaction with peptides can be greatly increased by a preliminary rapid alkaline hydrolysis (35). If the ninhydrin reaction is to be used to analyze fractions from columns developed in pyridine or collidine buffers, these solvents must be redistilled from a flask containing some ninhydrin to remove contaminants which react with it. If the Folin-Lowry reaction is to be used on fractions in pyridine or collidine buffers, the samples must be evaporated to dryness in order to remove pyridine and collidine, which interfere. This evaporation can be conveniently done by pipetting aliquots from the eluate fractions into test tubes, assembling the tubes into a vacuum desiccator, and pumping under high vacuum. Aliquots of 0.05 ml should be dry in about an hour, 0.1 ml aliquots in 4 hours. The ninhydrin, Folin-Lowry, Sakaguchi, and Pauly tests are all *p*H-sensitive, and due attention must be given to neutralization of excess acid or base.

Preparative paper chromatography

Although paper chromatography is most commonly used to ascertain the purity of peptides, it can be used to purify small amounts of peptides (1 to 50 mg or micromoles). If the peptide is found to be heterogeneous by paper chromatography, the solvent which has revealed its heterogeneity can be used to purify it.

SOLVENTS:
Solvents F, I, and M in Table 3 (p. 59) have often been used in preparative peptide separations. Pyridine may be purified as described by McDowell and Smith (68).

PROCEDURE FOR DEVELOPMENT:
The paper used for separating up to 15 mg (15 micromoles) of peptide is usually Whatman no. 1 or no. 4. Whatman 3 MM is used to separate larger quantities (up to 50 mg). The paper must be washed by overnight descending chromatography in the solvent to be used, and dried before use. Descending chromatography is preferable to ascending chromatography for preparative work, since longer times may be used and the resolution is superior. If the solvent is to be allowed to run off the sheet, serrate the bottom for more even dripping of solvent from the sheet. Apply the sample (which must be relatively salt-free) along the origin in 2 to 5 μl amounts per application and dry with a hairdrier before respotting. Put a spot of the peptide to be purified at either edge of the chromatogram as a marker. Some peptides stick to dry paper. If they are applied to paper and dried completely, they do not migrate, or migrate only partially from the origin. Such peptides are spotted in the chamber after the developing solvent has already wet the origin, or are applied to the paper and not completely dried before development with solvent.

LOCATION AND ELUTION OF PEPTIDES:
After solvent development, remove the sheets, using plastic gloves, and air-dry them. Cut off the marker strips, and stain them for location of the bands (using one or more of the sprays listed on pp. 62–64). Cut the areas of paper bearing the desired peptides from the sheets and elute them. The eluting solvent is usually H_2O, 0.1 N NH_3, or 1 N HOAc. Either extract the strips with the eluting solvent or lay them onto wet, prewashed Whatman 3 MM paper wicks in chromatographic troughs, and elute the samples from the strips by descending chromatography overnight into beakers in an enclosed chamber. Check the completeness of the elution of the strips by an appropriate identifying reagent. The eluates, after filtration, are concentrated *in vacuo* or lyophilized.

ANALYTICAL TECHNIQUES

Amino acid analysis

Hydrolysis of peptide-resins and aminoacyl-resins. Transfer the resin to which the peptide or amino acid has been coupled to a tared 50- or 100-ml ⩐ 24/40 round-bottom flask. After reweighing, record the weight of the resin. For amino acid analyzers using 0.5 micromole samples, about 10 mg of resin is usually adequate. If the resin is not dry, as when portions of resin are removed after each coupling reaction, connect the flask to a high-vacuum pump using the ⩐ 24/40 connectors (Appendix B, item 30) and dry it to constant weight. Add to the flask 5 ml of peroxide-free dioxane and 5 ml of concentrated HCl. Fit the flask with an air condenser and, after refluxing overnight on a hot plate set at low heat, filter the hydrolysate quantitatively through a porcelain Buchner funnel containing a 1.5-cm Whatman no. 1 filter-paper disc directly into another 100-ml round-bottom flask by using an adapter (Appendix B, item 8). Evaporate the filtered hydrolysate to dryness on a rotary evaporator under reduced pressure. Some nonvolatile liquid residue will remain because of hydrolysis of part of the dioxane, but it will not interfere with the amino acid analysis. If the peptide contains Glu or Gln, rehydrolyze the hydrolysate for 24 hours using 10 ml of 6 N HCl in order to obtain a proper analysis for this amino acid. These amino acids form esters with the alcohols produced by partial hydrolysis of dioxane. In the 50% dioxane medium, the equilibrium point of this esterification favors ester formation rather than hydrolysis. (Even on rehydrolysis the glutamic acid value may sometimes still be lower than that obtained after cleavage from the resin.) If a second hydrolysis is used, again remove the HCl by rotary evaporation. Add several aliquots of water to the hydrolysate and evaporate in order to remove most of the HCl. Then dilute the sample appropriately with the pH 2.2 diluting buffer used for amino acid analysis.

Hydrolysis of peptides. Peptides are hydrolyzed by 6 N HCl, after cleavage from the resin, in the usual way, either in sealed tubes (22 hours at 110°) or in 50-ml ⩐ 24/40 round-bottom flasks on a hot plate set at low heat (refluxed overnight). Using the latter technique, the final volume of the sample during hydrolysis should be at least 10 ml, since the peptide may be charred if the volume is too low.

Nitroarginine, on hydrolysis, yields arginine, ornithine, and NO_2-arginine, and the arginine content is calculated from the sum of these three amino acids. On the Spinco 120B Amino Acid Analyzer equipped with the AA15 and AA35 resins, ornithine appears at the position of lysine on the short column and nitroarginine at the buffer change from first buffer to second buffer on the long column. If only NO_2-arginine is on the resin, all 3 products can be satisfactorily determined by a single short-column (basic amino acids) run, taking the neutral peak as NO_2-arginine and adding it to the ornithine and arginine. In lieu of determining actual constants by using NO_2-Arg and Orn standards, the constant for NO_2-Arg may be taken as 0.866 times the average constant of the analyzer and that for Orn as 1.14 times the average constant. These and other amino acid derivatives, with their respective constants and times of emergence from the amino acid analyzer, are given in Table 1.

Certain amino acids may undergo serious loss during hydrolysis. In peptides containing both tyrosine and nitroarginine, mutual loss of these residues may occur. The low value obtained for glutamic acid in dioxane-HCl hydrolysates of peptide-resins has already been mentioned. Amino acids which are susceptible to oxidation (serine, threonine, tyrosine, cysteine, methionine) may be partially destroyed during hydrolysis. Peptides containing such residues should be hydrolyzed in evacuated sealed tubes.

The evacuation is done as follows. Place the peptide, dissolved in 6 N HCl (1 to 3 ml), in a 6-inch test tube. Soften the tube near the mouth in a flame and draw it out so that a narrow

TABLE 1.
Analysis of some common amino acid derivatives.[a]

Compound	Constant	Emergence time
Long column for acidic and neutral amino acids (*p*H 3.28 to 4.25):		
Cysteic acid	20.5	18 min.
Met sulfoxide	20.3	42 min. (just before Asp)
Nitro-Arg	18.5	138 min. (near buffer change)
O-Me-Tyr	17.5	35 min. after Phe
S-Bzl-Cys	16.3	45 min. after Phe
Tos-Arg	15.2	75 min. after Phe
Short column for basic amino acids (*p*H 5.28):		
Dnp-His	–	14 min.
ε-Tos-Lys	28.5	17.5 min.
Orn	24.4	18 min. (with lysine)
Trp	17.5	20 min.
im-Bzl-His	19.5	10 min. after buffer change[b]

[a] This table is for a Spinco Model 120B Amino Acid Analyzer, equipped for 4-hour analysis of protein hydrolysates. The average constant for this instrument is 21.37. The following formula may be used to estimate constants for these derivatives on another analyzer (B):

$$\text{Constant on analyzer B} = \left(\frac{\text{constant from Table 1}}{21.37}\right) \times \begin{array}{l}\text{(average constant of}\\\text{analyzer B).}\end{array}$$

[b] For Bzl-His, the short column is changed at 20 min. to a *p*H 7.0, 0.38 *M* buffer.

constriction is formed. Freeze the sample in a bath of Dry Ice and propanol. Connect the tube to a well-trapped vacuum pump and evacuate. Cautiously allow the frozen sample to warm just until all the ice is melted. During the melting, swirl the tube gently, holding it with the fingers just above the solution level (the warmth prevents a solvent bubble from rising up the tube), and hold the hose to the vacuum system so that it can be closed off instantaneously if bubbling gets out of control. Refreeze the sample and seal off the tube at the constriction, still under vacuum.

Sensitive amino acids can sometimes be protected by adding 0.1% phenol or mercaptoethanol to the acid before hydrolysis (109).

Tryptophan is usually completely destroyed by acid hydrolysis, and other methods of hydrolysis must be used, such as alkaline hydrolysis (see p. 49) or the enzymatic method described next.

Total enzymic hydrolysis using papain and aminopeptidase M (46).

REAGENTS:

1. Buffer for papain incubation—0.05 *M* ammonium acetate, *p*H 5.3.
2. Papain, 0.5 mg per ml, in H_2O.
3. Mercaptoethanol, 1:32 dilution in H_2O.
4. Buffer for Aminopeptidase M incubation—0.2 *M* trimethylamine acetate, *p*H 8.2.
5. Aminopeptidase M (APM) 10.0 mg per ml, in H_2O.

PROCEDURE:

Dry approximately 0.1 mg of polypeptide substrate in the bottom of a conical centrifuge tube. Add 85 μl of reagent 1 and 5 μl of reagent 3, giving a mercaptoethanol concentration of 0.02 *M* during digestion. Add 10 μl of reagent 2 (5 μg of papain) to the buffered substrate, providing a papain concentration of 50 μg per ml (enzyme-substrate ratio, 1:20, wt for wt) in a volume of 100 μl. Incubate the mixture at 37° for 2 hours, then inactivate the papain with 2 drops of HOAc and lyophilize the solution. Lyophilization is complete in 30 to 60 min. because of the small volume.

Next dissolve the partially digested mixture in 80 μl of reagent 4 and 5 μl of reagent 3. Add 15 μl of reagent 5 (150 μg of APM), giving a concentration of 1.5 mg per ml of APM (enzyme-substrate ratio, 1.5:1, wt for wt), again in a volume of 100 μl. Carry out the APM digestion for 3 hours, lower the pH with HOAc, and lyophilize the mixture. It may then be taken up directly in the appropriate volume of amino acid analyzer buffer for application to the column.

For polypeptides larger than 80 to 90 residues (such as ribonuclease), it is necessary to use a larger APM concentration for a somewhat longer time. Thus, 300 μg of APM are used for 3 hours, then a second 300 μg aliquot is added, and the incubation carried out three more hours; yields are then as satisfactory as those obtained with the smaller peptides.

Amino acids from autodigestion of the enzymes (determined in separate enzyme blanks) amount to less than 0.002 micromoles (and less than 0.0005 micromoles for most residues). In the presence of substrate, autodigestion is even less.

The method has been shown to effect quantitative recovery of asparagine, glutamine, tryptophan, cystine, trifluoroacetyl lysine, mono- and di-iodotyrosine, and nitroarginine, which are normally altered in acid hydrolysis. In the presence of the mercaptoethanol concentrations used, methionine and methionine sulfoxide are retained in their original state.

Chloride analysis by the
modified Volhard method (33)

PRINCIPLE:

The sample is acidified with HNO_3 and the chloride is precipitated with a measured excess of standard $AgNO_3$ solution. The AgCl that is formed is coated with toluene and the excess $AgNO_3$ is back-titrated with standard NH_4SCN solution, using ferric alum $(FeNH_4(SO_4)_2 \cdot 12H_2O)$ as an indicator. A red color, due to the formation of $Fe(SCN)_3$, indicates that an excess of SCN^- is present and that the end point has been reached.

REAGENTS:

1. Standard $AgNO_3$ (0.1 N = 16.989 g per l).
2. Standard NH_4SCN (0.1 N = 7.612 g per l). Since the NH_4SCN must be standardized against $AgNO_3$, so that 1.0 ml of NH_4SCN equals 1.0 ml of standard $AgNO_3$, prepare a slightly more concentrated solution of NH_4SCN and dilute it to 0.1 N after titration. The titration procedure is the same as described below, except that no sample is added. Calculate the amount of H_2O that should be added to the NH_4SCN to make 10 ml of the NH_4SCN exactly equivalent to 10 ml of $AgNO_3$. Repeat the procedure in the presence of a known concentration of NaCl (1 ml of 1 N NaCl) to check the test.
3. NaCl (1 N = 58.45 g per l).
4. Saturated ferric alum (124 g of $NH_4Fe(SO_4)_2 \cdot 12H_2O$ in 100 ml H_2O).
5. Toluene.
6. HNO_3 (1 N).

PROCEDURE:

Pipet a sample of standard NaCl solution into about 10 ml of H_2O in a 250-ml Erlenmeyer flask and protect from bright light. For titration of HCl-HOAc, use a 1 ml sample. To the flask add about 3 drops of reagent 4 and 1 ml of 1 N HNO_3. Put a magnetic stirring bar in the flask and place it on a magnetic stirrer. Slowly add 20 ml of standard $AgNO_3$, with stirring. Stop the stirrer and let the mixture stand for 5 min. Add about 50 ml of water, followed by toluene, so that about a $\frac{1}{4}$-inch layer of toluene is made on the water surface. Mix well with the stirrer. With the stirrer on, titrate with standard

NH₄SCN solution. The first permanent tinge of red-brown indicates the end-point.

CALCULATION:

For HCl-HOAc, [20 − (ml of NH₄SCN)] × 0.1 = N of HCl in HOAc.

When the Volhard method is used to determine chloride in solutions containing organic solvents other than acetic acid, results are better if the sample is diluted with 50 ml of HOAc before any reagents are added (77).

Quantitative Sakaguchi determination of arginine (138)

The Sakaguchi reaction gives a red color from unsubstituted or monosubstituted guanidines; more highly substituted guanidines do not react. Therefore arginine and arginine peptides give a positive reaction, while blocked arginines (e.g., nitro, tosyl) and their peptides are negative. The reaction is useful for following the hydrogenolysis of nitroarginine and for locating arginine peptides in CCD and chromatography.

SOLUTIONS:

1. Unknown: samples of peptide solutions or aliquots taken before and after hydrogenation of peptide, diluted with MeOH-H₂O (1:9) to contain 0.02 to 0.1 micromole of Arg per ml.
2. Standard: arginine, 0.05 micromole per ml (8.70 mg per liter); use 0.1 to 2.0 ml, and make up to 2.0 ml with water.

REAGENTS:

1. Dissolve 1 mg of α-naphthol per ml of MeOH, then dilute 1:5 with water, to give 0.02% α-naphthol in 20% MeOH (good for about 2 months).
2. A 2.5 N solution of NaOH.
3. NaOBr, prepared by dissolving 0.67 ml of Br₂ in 100 ml of 1 N NaOH (good for 2 weeks).
4. A 40% solution of urea in H₂O.

PROCEDURE:

To 2 ml of the standard or unknown solution, add 0.4 ml of reagent 2 (an acidic sample may need more NaOH; the solution must be strongly basic) plus 0.4 ml of reagent 1. Mix and chill in an ice bath. Add 0.04 ml of reagent 3; mix and immediately add 0.4 ml of reagent 4. Mix and read at 515 mμ (optimum color is obtained 20 seconds after addition of reagent 3). Although 5 μg of arginine hydrochloride gives an absorbance of 0.2, the molar extinction coefficient obtained from arginine in peptides may be much lower than that of free arginine. For example, the color yield of bradykinin is only about 70% of that expected, and some proteins have been reported to give color yields as low as 20%.

Quantitative Pauly determination of histidine and tyrosine

Histidine and tyrosine, either free or in peptide linkage, couple with diazotized sulfanilic acid to give a red product. This reagent is particularly useful for following the deprotection of the imidazole nucleus of histidine, since blocked imidazoles do not react.

REAGENTS:

1. Sodium nitrite, 5% in H₂O.
2. Sulfanilic acid, 0.5% in dilute HCl (5 ml concentrated HCl + 95 ml H₂O). (Store these two reagents in the cold, and use while cold.)
3. Sodium carbonate, 10% in H₂O.

PROCEDURE:

Mix in the cold equal parts of reagents 1 and 2, and let stand at least 5 min. To 1 ml of sample (must not be strongly acidic or basic), add 1 ml of reagent 3 and 1 ml of the mixed reagents. Read immediately at 500 mμ.

If alcohol is present in the sample it causes a yellow background which interferes, and better results can be obtained by reading at 520 mμ, although the values are lower.

Ammonia also interferes, and must be removed by alkaline evaporation.

When read immediately, 2 μg of histidine dihydrochloride or 10 μg of tyrosine gives an absorbance of 0.1 at 500 mμ. Color develops to a maximum 30 seconds after addition of the diazotized sulfanilic acid, fades in 3 min. to approximately half the density, then is stable for 15 min.

Determination of peptides by the Folin-Lowry method (58)

The Folin-Lowry color reaction is very useful for determining the presence of peptides. It is most sensitive for long peptides containing phenolic groups, but small nonaromatic peptides can also be detected. It has the advantage over ninhydrin of being easier to prepare, not requiring a heating step, and NH$_3$ does not interfere. Pyridine and collidine do interfere, and if present must be removed by drying the sample. The pH of the sample must be close to neutrality. The color curve is not linear; for accurate determinations of concentrations, a standard curve must be made (see Table 2).

REAGENTS:
1. Na$_2$CO$_3$, 2% in 0.1 N NaOH.
2. CuSO$_4$·5H$_2$O, 1% in H$_2$O.

3. Sodium potassium tartrate, 2% in H$_2$O.
4. Combine 0.5 ml of reagent 2 and 0.5 ml of reagent 3, and make up to 50 ml with reagent 1. Make up fresh each day.
5. Dilute commercially available Folin-Ciocalteau phenol reagent (1:1) with water (it should then be 1 N in HCl).

PROCEDURE:

To between 0.05 and 0.2 ml of the sample, add 3 ml of reagent 4 and let stand 10 min. Run a reagent blank at the same time. Add 0.3 ml reagent 5, with shaking. After 30 min. read the color at 700 mμ. Subtract the reagent blank. The volumes can be modified as long as the proportion of reagent 4 to reagent 5 is 10:1. If the sample volume is too high, the volume of the reaction mixture can be reduced by preparing reagent 4 at double strength and using 1.5 ml of it to 0.3 ml of reagent 5, or by decreasing the volumes of the normal reagents 4 and 5 to 1.0 and 0.1 ml, respectively.

The quantitative ninhydrin reaction (87)

The ninhydrin assay for quantitative estimation of peptides is useful for small peptides, for peptides containing a high percentage of lysine

TABLE 2.
Representative color values from the Folin-Lowry reaction.

Material	Amount of material and final volume of Folin reagent	Absorbance at 700 mμ	Absorbance for 1 mg in 1 ml of Folin reagent
Tobacco mosaic virus protein, 18 mg per micromole	0.04 mg in 2.4 ml	0.343	22.6
TMV protein tryptic peptide 8 (20 amino acids), 2.2 mg per micromole	0.01 micromole in 1.1 ml	0.567	31.1
Leu-Asp-Ala-Thr-Arg, 0.57 mg per micromole	0.1 micromole in 1.1 ml	0.71	13.7

residues, or for large peptides after a preliminary rapid alkaline hydrolysis (35). To carry out this hydrolysis, evaporate aliquots to dryness in polypropylene test tubes in an oven. To each tube add 0.15 ml of 13.5 N NaOH, and autoclave the tubes for 20 min. at 15 psi. Neutralize the alkali in the cooled tubes by adding 0.25 ml of HOAc to each one.

If the ninhydrin analysis will be used for samples in pyridine-containing buffers, the pyridine must be distilled from ninhydrin before use. If samples in ammonia buffers are to be used, the samples must be made strongly alkaline with NaOH and evacuated in a desiccator for some time (or evaporated to dryness in an oven) to remove the ammonia, and then neutralized with an equivalent amount of acetic acid before analysis. Samples must not contain more acid or base than can be neutralized to pH 5 by 1 ml of 0.1 N base or acid, otherwise the color formation will be inhibited.

REAGENTS:

1. Sodium acetate buffer, pH 5.5, 4 M. Dissolve 2720 g of NaOAc·3H$_2$O in 3 liters of water by warming. Cool to 25°, add 500 ml HOAc, and make up to 5 liters with water. Adjust pH to 5.51. Store at 4° without preservative.
2. Ninhydrin reagent. Dissolve 20 g ninhydrin and 3 g hydrindantin in 750 ml of peroxide-free methyl cellosolve (cellosolve should not give more than a light straw color when mixed 2 to 1 with 4% KI solution). Do not shake or stir vigorously, or the hydrindantin will be oxidized by the air. Add 250 ml of reagent 1, bubble nitrogen through the reagent for several minutes, and store in a dark bottle under nitrogen. The reagent is good for about a week. Many investigators find it more convenient to make up each time just the amount needed, without bothering with the nitrogen aeration and storage. For greater convenience, a table can be made, showing the amounts of the different components needed for various quantities of reagent.

PROCEDURE:

For 1- or 2-ml fractions, use 1 ml of reagent 2. Do not neutralize if less than 1 ml of 0.1 N NaOH or HCl will give pH 4-6. After addition of the reagent, mix gently by swirling, and cap tubes loosely. Heat for 15 min. in a boiling water bath, and cool immediately. Add 5 ml of 50% EtOH to each tube, and shake well to air-oxidize the remaining hydrindantin (this gives a more stable baseline). Tubes are read at 570 mμ, except for N-terminal proline or hydroxyproline peptides, which are read at 440 mμ, or at the absorption maximum, if different. The standard is leucine, at 50 μg per ml; 0.2 ml of this solution gives an absorbance of 0.2.

Paper and thin-layer chromatography

Paper chromatography (123). Paper chromatography, although not so rapid as TLC, is very useful for characterizing and estimating the purity of peptides. Chromatography may be done by either the ascending or the descending method; Whatman no. 1 paper is generally used. Some of the solvents which are commonly used for peptides are given in Table 3. Strongly acidic (formic acid) and basic systems should be used with caution, since they may cause degradation of some peptides. (For identification sprays, see pp. 62–64.) The relative mobilities of peptides in several of the solvents are given in the subsection on TLC of peptides.

Thin-layer chromatography (49, 96, 126). Thin-layer chromatography is useful for estimating the purity both of starting materials for SPPS and of synthesized peptides. TLC plates may be spread using Brinkman Silica Gel G or Silica Gel H; both give essentially the same Rf's. Precoated glass plates, coated plastic sheets, plastic sheets or glass plates coated with cellulose powder, and other media and equipment for TLC are commercially available.

Plastic sheets are laid against glass plates to hold them erect during solvent development. An advantage of the sheets is that they may be cut after chromatography so that several identifying sprays can easily be used. For chromatographing one or two spots, they can be cut into narrow strips and developed in large test tubes.

The solvents which have been useful for TLC of amino acid derivatives and peptides are given in Table 3. The atmosphere in the developing chamber must be fully saturated with the solvent, or Rf's will not be reproducible. Sheets of filter paper moistened with the solvent and stuck to the walls of the chamber help saturate the atmosphere. Standards should always be run along with unknowns if possible.

TLC OF AMINO ACID DERIVATIVES. The amino acid derivatives used in SPPS must be of high purity. Every order received, even of the same lot number, should be checked for its purity by TLC.

Spot approximately 1 μl of the amino acid derivative solution (10 to 50 mg per ml in CH_2Cl_2 or EtOAc) on TLC plates and run in several of the solvents given in Table 3. Assess the purity of Boc amino acids by spraying the developed chromatograms with ninhydrin both before and after deprotection of the Boc group in HCl vapor (see p. 62). The chlorine peptide spray and other sprays for identification of certain groups are also useful for certain derivatives. Approximate Rf's of a number of derivatives in the various solvents are given in

TABLE 3.
Solvents for TLC and paper chromatography.

| Solvent[a] | Amino acid derivatives, TLC silica gel | Peptides | |
		TLC silica gel	TLC cellulose or paper
A. Chloroform (85), methanol (10), acetic acid (5)	x		
B. Chloroform (95), acetic acid (5)	x		
C. Acetone (98), acetic acid (2)	x		
D. Chloroform (90), methanol (8), acetic acid (2)	x		
E. Chloroform (5), acetone (1)	x		
F. 1-Butanol (15), acetic acid (3), water (12), pyridine (10)	x	x	x P[b]
G. 1-Propanol (84), concentrated ammonium hydroxide (37)	x		
H. Isopropyl ether (6), acetic acid (1), chloroform (3)	x		
I. 1-Butanol (4), acetic acid (1), water (1)		x	x P
J. Phenol (88% liquefied, 3), water (1)		x	x
K. 1-Propanol (2), water (1)			x
L. Pyridine (4), water (1)			x
M. Isoamyl alcohol (7), pyridine (7), water (6)			x P
N. Pyridine (50), acetic acid (30), water (15)		x	x
O. 2-Butanone (10), acetic acid (30), water (25)		x	x
P. Ethyl acetate (5), pyridine (5), acetic acid (1), water (3)		x	
Q. 1-Butanol (65 ml), isopropanol (15 ml), water (20 ml), chloroacetic acid (3 g)		x	x

[a] Parts by volume except where indicated otherwise.
[b] P designates that the solvent is often used in preparative paper chromatography of peptides.

TABLE 4.

Rf's of Boc amino acids after TLC in various solvents on Silica Gel G.

Boc amino acid	Solvent[a]							
	A	B	C	D	E	F	G	H
alanine	0.61	0.30	0.75					0.55
nitroarginine	0.30	0.00	0.54					0.06
asparagine	0.21	0.38	0.69					
aspartic β-benzyl ester	0.78	0.29	0.76					
S-benzyl cysteine	0.73	0.42	0.73					
glutamic γ-benzyl ester	0.76	0.22	0.78					
glutamic γ-*p*-nitrobenzyl ester	0.83	0.23						
glutamine	0.36	0.00	0.68					
glycine	0.65	0.21	0.65					0.41
im-benzyl histidine	0.15	0.00	0.09					
im-DNP histidine	0.55							
isoleucine	0.68	0.42	0.73					0.60
leucine	0.70	0.33	0.81					0.64
ε-carbobenzoxy lysine	0.73	0.17	0.68					
α-carbobenzoxy lysine	0.66					0.66	0.66	
methionine	0.69	0.30	0.67					0.54
phenylalanine	0.70	0.39	0.85					0.59
proline	0.63	0.31	0.75					0.51
O-benzyl serine	0.74	0.39	0.70		0.00		0.51	
threonine	0.38	0.04	0.48					0.28
O-benzyl threonine	0.77							
tryptophan	0.50	0.19						0.44
O-benzyl tyrosine	0.77	0.37	0.78	0.50				
valine	0.73	0.39	0.86					0.65

[a]See Table 3 for solvent composition.

Tables 4 and 5. Spotting the derivatives at a low level gives the correct Rf; high levels show the presence of impurities.

TLC OF PEPTIDES.   Excellent results have been obtained with cellulose-powder-coated sheets and plates as well as with silica gel plates and sheets. In comparison with paper chromatography, the development times are short (1 or 2 hours) and the small, nondiffused spots give very high resolution and sensitivity. The solvent systems used for paper chromatography are used for cellulose TLC. Some solvents recom-mended for these and for silica-gel TLC of peptides are given in Table 3. Solvents N, O, P, and Q were recommended by D. Nitecki. Solvent N is for slow-moving compounds; O is the most satisfactory of all the solvents and is very good for fingerprinting. It is about three times faster than 1-butanol-containing solvents. Solvent P is a very fast polar solvent and is suitable only for TLC (not paper). Solvent Q gives about the same mobilities as solvent I, but gives better resolution and is very good for diastereoisomer separations. The migration of peptides in these solvents (relative to the commonly used solvent I) is as follows (91), for neutral unblocked peptides: N > O > P > I = Q. For very acidic peptides, the relative mobilities are different on paper than on silica gel TLC: for paper, O > N > I = Q ≫ P; for silica gel, N > O > P = I.

Paper electrophoresis (146)

Purity of peptides may be conveniently checked by paper electrophoresis as well as by paper chromatography and amino acid analysis; it is especially useful for peptides containing charged amino acids. Preparative electrophoresis may also be performed, using techniques similar to those described for paper chromatography. A power supply which will furnish 1000 volts at 50 ma is adequate, and can be used for most peptides without cooling. A convenient system uses sheets of Whatman no. 1 filter paper, 4.5×22.5 in., sandwiched between pieces of $\frac{1}{4} \times 5 \times 18$ in. plate glass. Up to six spots can be applied to such paper strips. Hold the plates together with large office clips (Hunt Clip #4), using four on each side. Before first being used, treat the sides of the glass plates which face the paper to make them water-repellent, by rubbing them with silicone grease; wipe off excess grease. Dip the paper in the buffer, blot well between filter-paper sheets, and spot with the samples, using 1 to 10 μl. Always apply a reference mixture containing picric acid, alanine, aspartic acid, and arginine (1 mg per ml of each) to the sheet. The picric acid provides a visual indication of the progress of the electrophoresis during the run. Rest the ends of the glass plate sandwich on the buffer wells or place a support under the sandwich. Dip the ends of the paper into the buffer wells, making certain that the buffer is at the same level in each well. The time of electrophoresis is 1 or 2 hours at 1000 v, or the time required for picric acid to travel 10 cm from the origin. The *p*H 6.4 buffer has a strong pyridine odor and should be used in the hood. After the current is turned off, remove the sheets from the sandwich and air-dry in a hood. Locate the materials by an appropriate spray. Remove the buffer from the buffer wells, and rinse and drain the wells after each use, especially if they are made of plastic. The buffer may be used several times.

BUFFERS:
1. *p*H 1.9: 88% formic acid (15), acetic acid (10), water (75).

TABLE 5.

Rf's of Boc amino acid p-nitrophenyl esters after TLC on silica Gel G.

Amino acid nitrophenyl ester	Solvent system[a]		
	A	B	C
Boc asparagine	0.63	0.15	0.69
Boc aspartic-β-benzyl ester	0.95	0.60	0.99
Boc glutamic-γ-benzyl ester	0.95	0.58	0.95
Boc glutamine	0.65	0.15	0.75
Boc glycine	0.89	0.55	0.99
Di-Z-histidine	–	0.00	–
Boc phenylalanine	0.95	0.59	1.00
Boc O-benzyl serine	0.95	0.59	1.00

[a]See Table 3 for solvent composition.

2. *p*H 2.8: 1 *M* acetic acid.
3. *p*H 3.6: pyridine (1), acetic acid (10), water (90).
4. *p*H 5.6: pyridine (2.3), acetic acid (0.6), water (97).
5. *p*H 6.4: pyridine (10), acetic acid (0.4), water (90).
6. *p*H 7–9: tris (hydroxymethyl) aminomethane, 0.05 *M*.

All proportions are in parts by volume.

Identification sprays

The following sprays are useful in identifying amino acids, amino acid derivatives, and peptides. The Sakaguchi spray cannot be used for silica gel TLC plates, but the other sprays can be used for both paper and TLC. (For additional spray reagents, see 96, 123, 126, 146.) Some identifying sprays can be used sequentially, so that a maximum amount of information can be obtained from a single spot (see 24). The sample sizes indicated are those usually spotted for chromatography or electrophoresis. Spots on chromatograms will diffuse and run if the reagent is applied too heavily and the substance spotted is soluble in the reagent. Aqueous reagents should be sprayed very lightly onto chromatograms that bear amino acids or peptides. Dipping is useable only if the chromatographed materials are totally insoluble in the reagent.

Deprotection of Boc amino acids before ninhydrin staining. Dry the TLC sheets or plates after solvent development, and place them in a closed chamber containing a beaker of fresh, concentrated HCl. After 15 min. of exposure to the HCl fumes, heat the plates for 10 min. in a 105° oven. Spray the plates with the buffered ninhydrin reagent while warm; colors usually develop immediately.

Buffered ninhydrin reagent. Spray chromatograms with (or, for paper, dip in) a mixture of acetic acid (3 ml), pyridine (1.5 ml), acetone (96 ml), and ninhydrin (10 mg). After the spray has dried, place the chromatogram in an oven at 105° for 5 min. The ninhydrin reagent should be made fresh each day. The pyridine should be distilled from a flask containing ninhydrin before use. For samples of amino acids, use 1 microliter of 1 mg per ml; for peptides, use increasing amounts in proportion to the chain length.

Unbuffered ninhydrin reagent. A more stable unbuffered reagent, which is adequate for many chromatograms but does not show as many distinguishing colors as the above spray, is a 0.2% solution of ninhydrin in acetone, which is stable for long periods if it is kept refrigerated.

Chlorine peptide spray (92). This spray is very useful for protected peptides not visible with ninhydrin, as well as for detecting impurities both in amino acid derivatives and in peptides. A positive reaction is given by almost all compounds which contain N–H groups. All alcohol and acids must be removed from the chromatogram prior to its use. It fails if dioxane has been used for solvent development. Some TLC plates containing a fluorescent indicator have also inhibited the color development.

REAGENTS:
1. Freshly diluted commercial Clorox in H_2O, 1:10 by volume.
2. Ethanol, 95%.
3. 1% KI in H_2O.
4. Freshly prepared *o*-tolidine in 1.5 *M* acetic acid. Mix the *o*-tolidine (about 100 mg to 10 ml of 10% HOAc) and filter through Whatman no. 1 filter paper.

Alternatively, instead of reagents 3 and 4, a solution of 1% soluble starch and 1% KI in water may be used. Bring the water to a boil, and add the soluble starch. Cool the solution to room temperature, and add the KI and dissolve.

PROCEDURE:

S̶̶ ... ̶d̶r̶i̶e̶d̶ ̶p̶l̶a̶t̶e̶s̶ ̶o̶r̶ sheets

cause purple backgrounds. Too long a drying time or too much EtOH will cause faint spots.

A very elegant alternative to reagents 1 and 2 is to spray the chromatogram with a 1% solution of *t*-butyl hypochlorite in cyclohexane (67). The excess of this volatile reagent evaporates readily. This modification has been very useful on silica gel TLC.

Identification of p-nitrophenyl esters. The yellow color of *p*-nitrophenyl esters is intensified by lightly spraying the dried plates with 1 *N* ammonium hydroxide or 0.5 *M* Na₂CO₃.

Sakaguchi spray for arginine (not for silica gel plates).

REAGENTS:
1. 8-hydroxyquinoline or α-naphthol, 0.1% in acetone.
2. NaOBr (0.67 ml Br₂ in 100 ml 1 *N* NaOH).

PROCEDURE:
   Dip paper through reagent 1 and air-dry. Lightly spray with reagent 2. Arginine-containing materials are bright orange, fading rapidly. The spots must be outlined immediately with a red pencil or a marking pencil which will write on wet paper. A more sensitive spray, which gives permanent colors, is described by Irrevere (41). Use 1 to 5 microliters of sample containing about 1 mg per ml

equivalent of arginine. Color yield may be very low in peptides.

...*ly spray (tyrosine and histidine).*

...NTS:
...fanilic acid, 9 g in 90 ml of concentrated ...Cl.
...NO₂, 5% in water.
...₂CO₃, 10% in water.
...ore reagents 1 and 2 in the cold (4°).

...EDURE:
   Mix 10 ml cold reagent 1 and 10 ml cold reagent 2, and let stand at a temperature below 20° for 5 min. Add 20 ml reagent 3 and spray chromatogram lightly. Tyrosine stains pink, histidine orange. Substituents on the imidazole ring of histidine inhibit the color formation. Use 1 to 5 microliters of samples containing about 1 mg per ml equivalent of tyrosine or histidine.

Nitrosonaphthol reagent for tyrosine (123).

REAGENTS:
1. 1-nitroso-2-naphthol, 0.1% in EtOH (acetone *not* recommended).
2. HNO₃, concentrated (70%).

PROCEDURE:
   Immediately before use, combine reagent 1 with reagent 2 (9:1) and dip or spray the chromatogram. Let dry 2 or 3 min. at room temperature, then heat 2 or 3 min. at 105°. Tyrosine gives a red color. The spots fade if the heating is prolonged.

Ehrlich spray for tryptophan.

REAGENTS:
1. *p*-dimethylamino benzaldehyde, 10% in concentrated HCl.
2. Acetone.

PROCEDURE:

In a hood, combine before use reagent 1 with reagent 2 (1:4), and spray or dip the chromatogram. Tryptophan-containing materials turn purple after several minutes.

Iodine. Many organic compounds give brown colors when exposed to iodine vapor. Spread iodine crystals on a watch glass in a closed jar and let stand until the jar is filled with vapor. Immerse plates or sheets in the vapor for 5 or 10 min. The brown colors fade rapidly, but can be fixed by spraying with a 1% starch solution after excess I_2 has evaporated.

3

APPARATUS USED IN
SOLID PHASE SYNTHESIS

SPECIAL GLASSWARE

Reaction vessels

The reaction vessel originally described by Merrifield (71) is shown in Figure 24. This vessel, in the three sizes indicated, has been widely used and found to be generally satisfactory. When it is used with a rocking device which provides 105° rotation (clockwise from the position shown in the figure), the resin is sufficiently agitated, and if the solvent is added properly (see p. 38), all the resin is satisfactorily washed and brought into reaction. This type of reaction vessel has also been constructed in a very large size (56) suitable for handling up to 50 g of resin, and a microvessel, consisting of a short piece of Teflon tubing shrunk down onto a small fritted disc, with a stopcock at one end and a 10/18 ground joint at the other, has been used (121) for handling a few milligrams of radioactive peptide-resins.

The system of Samuels and Holybee (see pp. 68–70) uses a vessel similar to the one on the Merrifield-Stewart automatic instrument, but with a rocker which provides complete inversion (180°) of the vessel. Enough of the solvents and reagents must always be used to fill the vessel more than half full, so that the walls of the vessel will always be thoroughly washed. This system does not allow coupling reactions to be carried out in very small amounts of solvents in order to accelerate the coupling and minimize side-reactions.

Khosla *et al.* have described a vessel for SPPS which is always kept upright (48). Solvents are added in such a way that the walls are washed down each time, and are removed by a sealed-in filter stick inserted from above and reaching almost to the bottom of the vessel. Mixing is by shaking, and liquids are added through a special funnel that does not require opening the vessel each time. The vessel may be too large (250 or 500 ml) for small batches of resin, and it may be difficult to remove the last traces of solvents by their filtering arrangement.

An upright stationary vessel has been described by Grahl-Nielsen and Tritsch (30). In their system, solvents are metered by measuring pipets and presumably are added in such a way that the entire inner wall of the vessel is washed. The resin is agitated by a motor-driven stirrer, and solvents are removed by suction through a sintered glass disc at the bottom of the vessel.

Sipos and Denning (122) have fitted a tilted (45°) rotary evaporator (Buchler PFE-IBN, continuous feed model) with a synthesis vessel. In operation, the vessel is rotated continually. Solvents and reagents are added through the feed tube at the top and are removed by suction through a magnetic valve below the fritted disc at the bottom of the vessel.

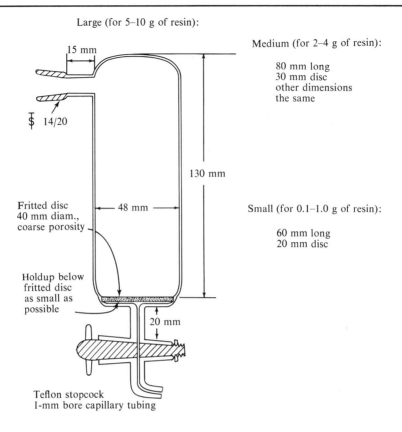

Large (for 5–10 g of resin):

15 mm

14/20

130 mm

Fritted disc
40 mm diam.,
coarse porosity

48 mm

Holdup below
fritted disc
as small as
possible

20 mm

Teflon stopcock
1-mm bore capillary tubing

Medium (for 2–4 g of resin):

80 mm long
30 mm disc
other dimensions
the same

Small (for 0.1–1.0 g of resin):

60 mm long
20 mm disc

FIGURE 24.
Reaction Vessels.

Many different satisfactory systems of glassware for SPPS could doubtless be devised, and each might possess certain advantages. We consider that an ideal vessel or system would: (1) allow for reasonable variation in batch size —at present different sizes of vessels are necessary; (2) provide for rapid and thorough suspension of the resin, so that all beads are in good contact with the solvent without being subjected to any grinding action, such as is caused by magnetic stirrers; (3) provide for rapid and convenient addition of solvents in such a way that vessel walls are washed down, unless this is provided for by the agitation system; (4) allow different solvent volumes to be used at will with equal efficiency of resin contact; (5) provide for convenient removal of resin samples during the synthesis; and (6) provide for rapid and complete solvent removal.

Cleavage vessels

Although the peptide can be cleaved from the resin with HBr-TFA in the synthesis vessel, it is generally preferable to remove the peptide-resin from the synthesis vessel and dry it before cleavage, since doing so allows the amount of peptide incorporated to be estimated from the weight gain, and also conveniently allows part of the peptide-resin to be stored for future use. The peptide can be conveniently cleaved from the resin with HBr-TFA in one of the vessels shown in Figure 25.

The larger of the two cleavage vessels shown in Figure 25 is particularly versatile. The tapered bottom allows very small amounts of peptide-resins to be handled satisfactorily, yet several grams may also be easily cleaved.

Maintenance of vessels

With continued use, the fritted glass filter disc of both synthesis and cleavage vessels will become clogged with fine resin particles. To prevent such clogging during a synthesis, the synthesis vessels should be routinely cleaned with hot chromic-sulfuric acid after each run of several residues. Adequate time should be allowed for thorough digestion of all resin particles; a measure of thorough cleaning is the persistence of the clear orange color of the cleaning solution. Cleavage vessels can be similarly cleaned whenever filtration begins to slow down. The vessels may be freed of resin particles by placing them in a glass blower's oven overnight rather than by using a cleaning solution. Discs made of glass beads rather than of the usual crushed glass will not become clogged with resin; such discs are available from Yeager. (A. Robinson.)

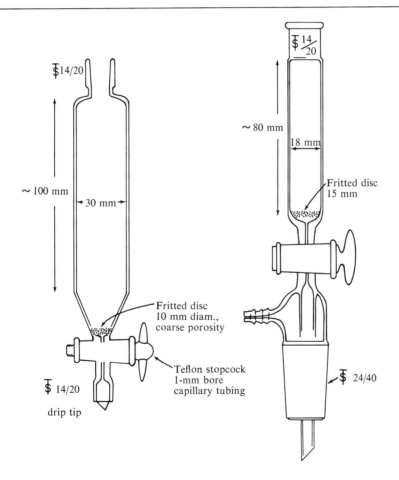

FIGURE 25.
Cleavage Vessels.

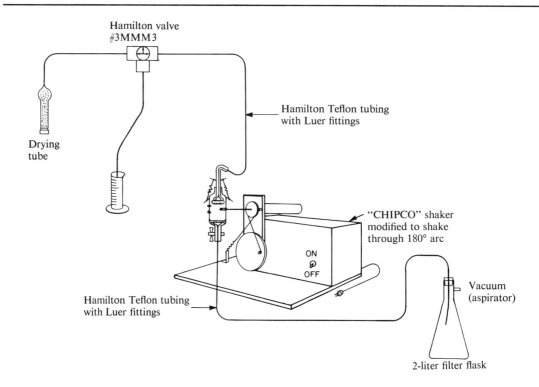

Hamilton valve
#3MMM3

Hamilton Teflon tubing
with Luer fittings

Drying
tube

"CHIPCO" shaker
modified to shake
through 180° arc

ON
OFF

Vacuum
(aspirator)

Hamilton Teflon tubing
with Luer fittings

2-liter filter flask

FIGURE 26.
The Samuels System (single valve).

The peptide shaker

The "shaker" originally designed (see Figure 18) at Rockefeller University for peptide synthesis (71, 128) is now commercially available in a modified form. This instrument rocks the glass vessel through an arc of 105° at about 25 cycles per minute. Faster rocking causes undue splashing of the resin suspension; slower rocking causes the resuspension of the resin after filtration to be rather slow. The ideal shaker should have a clutch, which would disengage the vessel from the motor when the power is removed, and provide enough friction to hold the vessel in any position in which it is stopped, but still allow the vessel to be rocked manually, so that solvents may be added conveniently. The shaker illustrated in Figure 18 is equipped with a Hurst PC-DA motor with electric clutch, which provides this desirable feature.

MANUAL SYSTEMS FOR SOLID PHASE PEPTIDE SYNTHESIS
(by Robert B. Samuels and Leslie D. Holybee)

Solid phase peptide synthesis may be carried out using simple, nonautomatic valving systems which eliminate some undesirable manipulations (such as opening the reaction flask to add reagents), and also reduce the addition time per residue to that achieved by automatic SPPS instruments. Examples of such systems are shown in Figures 26 and 27.

The simplest arrangement (Figure 26) consists of a reaction vessel similar to that used on the Merrifield-Stewart automatic instrument (81, 82), but with a 1-mm Teflon stopcock built into the lower part between the sintered disc and the male Luer fitting, a Mann Chipco shaker, and a Hamilton Teflon 3MMM3 valve.

The drying tube is fitted with a male Luer fitting, and the components are interconnected with Hamilton Teflon KF11TF tubing with attached Kel-F female Luer fittings. The Teflon tubing may be connected to the rubber stopper in the filter flask by pulling the tubing through an undersized hole in the stopper. The Chipco shaker, manufactured to swing the reaction vessel through an arc of 100°, is fitted with a Stephens action, enabling it to shake through a 180° arc, from vertical to vertical. This modification permits more thorough rinsing of the inner walls of the reaction vessel with each shaking cycle. (The tubing to and from the reaction vessel passes through the hollow arm of the shaker, but for improved clarity this detail was omitted from Figures 26 and 27.)

To operate, place the reaction vessel containing resin (substituted with the C-terminal residue) on the shaker in the inverted position (as in Figure 27) with the Teflon stopcock open. Turn on the water aspirator to create a vacuum in the filter flask, and measure the first solvent into the graduated cylinder. Turn the Hamilton valve so that the solution is drawn into the reaction vessel. As soon as the graduated cylinder is empty, turn the Hamilton valve to connect the drying tube (filled with Drierite or some other desiccant) with the reaction vessel, close the Teflon stopcock, and turn on the shaker. To prevent the solvent from backing up from the vessel into the filler line during shaking, turn the valve to seal off the line. During the shaking cycle, the operator can fill the graduated cylinder with the next solvent. Premeasured amounts of amino acid derivatives and DCC may be taken directly from small storage vials, avoiding the transfer to the graduated cylinder.

To remove solvent from the reaction vessel at the completion of the shaking step, turn off the shaker with the flask in the upright position,

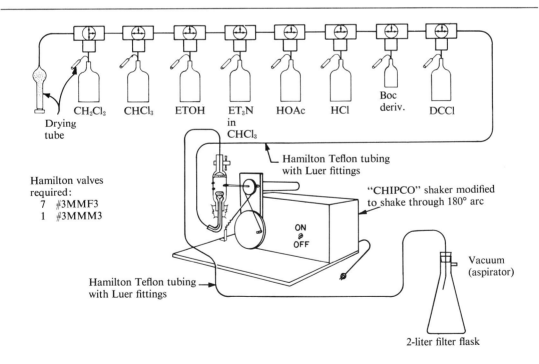

FIGURE 27.
The Samuels System (multiple valve).

turn the Hamilton valve to connect the drying tube to the vessel, and open the Teflon stopcock. To continue, invert the reaction vessel and repeat the filling procedure as described above.

The manipulations may be simplified further by expanding the system to include additional Hamilton valves and drying tubes (see Figure 27). A valve train is formed by connecting seven Hamilton 3MMF3 valves and one Hamilton 3MMM3 valve together, either directly or with interconnectors for less crowding of the control levers. The 3MMM3 valve should be the one at the extreme left in the figures, so that the drying tube can be attached to it via Teflon tubing and a Kel-F Luer cap.

The operation of this system is very similar to that of the system described above. To fill the reaction vessel, first invert it, open the appropriate valve to the solvent (as shown for methylene chloride in Figure 27), and open the Teflon stopcock on the reaction vessel. Volume is measured in this system by filling to predetermined markers on the reaction vessel itself. If the resin is thoroughly aspirated before the reaction vessel is refilled, the resin will adhere to the large fritted disc during the filling operation and will not interfere with the volume measurement. Make up the amino acid derivatives in a small volume of solvent and store them in individual one-shot vials, which can then be emptied to obtain the correct amount of derivative in the reaction vessel. The DCC may be similarly handled, or may be stored in a graduated reservoir from which known volumes may be accurately withdrawn as required. The use of a different-colored Teflon tubing for each solvent helps insure correct solvent selection. After shaking, stop the reaction vessel in the upright position and open the Teflon stopcock to permit removal of the liquid.

AUTOMATIC PEPTIDE SYNTHESIS (81, 82)

The fact that all the operations of SPPS are carried out in one vessel (after the first amino acid is attached to the resin), and involve only addition of liquid, agitation, and removal of liquid by filtration, makes the system suitable for automatic operation. An instrument that will carry out these operations has been described (81), and has been used to synthesize many peptides during the last three years. This instrument, once it has been loaded with an amino acid-resin and supplied with the proper solvents, reagents, and Boc amino acid solutions, will operate unattended for 24 hours, during which time it will lengthen the peptide on the resin by 6 amino acids. After the amino acid reservoirs have been rinsed and replenished with 6 new Boc amino acid solutions, the instrument is ready to continue the synthesis for another 24 hours. The instrument operates on either a DCC or an active-ester program, a separate program drum being used for each type of coupling reaction. This instrument has proved to be a great timesaver, especially in the synthesis of long peptides.

An improved version of this instrument has been constructed (see Frontispiece) and is now in operation in the laboratory (129). It provides for automatic selection of the type of coupling reaction and incorporates some additional safety devices and conveniences.

Several other automatic instruments for SPPS have been designed and built in different laboratories, and a description of one has been published by Robinson (101). They use various systems for selection, metering, and transfer of solvents and for agitation of the reaction vessel. It is not yet apparent which type of instrument will ultimately prove to be the best one for SPPS. Two different types of automatic SPPS instrument are currently being developed commercially, and should soon make automatic peptide synthesis available for many investigators (7, 115).

THE SCOPE
AND LIMITATIONS OF
SOLID PHASE SYNTHESIS

Research in the six years since the introduction of the solid phase method has developed methods suitable for incorporating all the naturally occurring amino acids, as well as several unnatural amino acids and other prosthetic groups, into peptides. Appendix F is a partial list of peptides synthesized by the solid phase method; chains of up to 55 amino acid residues have been satisfactorily made. It is not yet clear whether there will be any limitations on peptide length or not; it can only be stated that no limit has so far been reached.

We estimate that at least two hundred different peptides have so far been successfully synthesized by the solid phase method. Merrifield has published a complete list (76) of all those described in the literature before February 1967. His list details the solid support, protecting groups, coupling reagents, deprotection reagent, cleavage method, and purification technique used, as well as the yields obtained. Appendix F only indicates the scope of the applications of the method and adds some more recent examples.

However, the solid phase method is not black magic, and does not automatically guarantee a satisfactory outcome for every synthesis attempted. Methods which usually give complete coupling may well not do so with new classes of peptides or with long peptides or proteins, where secondary structural features may manifest themselves. Each researcher must demonstrate by unequivocal methods that the product he obtains from any synthesis is homogeneous and possesses the expected structure. For small peptides this proof is relatively simple, but for large peptides and proteins it is an entirely different matter. Simple amino acid analysis is not adequate, particularly when there are several residues of a given amino acid in the molecule. Also, the potency of biologically active peptides and proteins must be used with caution, since most bioassays are not overly accurate, and the effects on biological activity of deletions or substitutions of amino acids cannot usually be predicted with certainty. Adequate checks on the progress of the synthesis must be made frequently during the assembly of long chains, and if any difficulty in securing complete reactions is encountered, suitable methods for overcoming the difficulty must be developed before the synthesis can proceed. In general, the application of a range of criteria for purity and identity should help prevent unjustified claims from appearing in the literature.

Appendix A
ADDRESSES OF SUPPLIERS

Apparatus, glassware, and chemicals needed for SPPS may be purchased from the suppliers whose addresses are listed here. The name of the supplier used in Appendixes B and C is the part of the name italicized here.

Supplier, Address, and Telephone

1. *Aldrich* Chemical Co.
   2371 N. 30th Street
   Milwaukee, Wis. 53210
   (414) 374-4620

   78 Clinton Road
   Fairfield, N.J. 07006
   (201) 228-4750

   Wilshire Chemical Co.
   15324 S. Broadway
   Gardena, Calif.
   (213) 323-9232

2. J. T. *Baker* Co.[a,b]
   Phillipsburg, N. J. 08865
   (201) 859-2151

3. *Bel-Art* Products
   Pequannock, N.J. 07440
   (201) 694-0500

4. *Berkeley Glass* Laboratory
   1165 - 67th Street
   Oakland, Calif. 94608
   (415) 654-8616

5. *Bio-Rad* Laboratories
   32nd and Griffin Avenues
   Richmond, Calif. 94804
   (415) 234-4130

   22 Jones Street
   New York, N.Y. 10014
   (212) 929-4823

6. *Brinkmann* Instruments, Inc.[a]
   Westbury, N.Y. 11590
   (516) 334-7500

7. *Buchler* Instruments
   1327 16th Street
   Fort Lee, N.J. 07025
   (201) 945-1188

8. *Cal-Glass* (formerly Lab Glass, Inc.)[a]
   3012 Enterprise Street
   Costa Mesa, Calif. 92626
   (213) 625-1121 or (714) 546-7250

9. C. E. *Conover* and Co.
   333 Passaic Avenue
   Fairfield, N.J. 07006
   (201) 228-1400

10. *Cyclo* Chemical Corp.
    1922 East 64th Street
    Los Angeles, Calif. 90001
    (213) 581-8221

    1133 Broadway
    New York, N.Y. 10010
    (212) 255-4640

11. *Eastman* Organic Chemicals[b]
    Distillation Products Industries
    Eastman Organic Chemicals Department
    Rochester, N.Y. 14603
    (716) 458-4080

12. *Engelhard* Industries
    113 Astor Street
    Newark, N.J. 07114
    (201) 242-2700

13. *Fisher* Scientific Co.[a,b]
    Springfield, N.J.
    (201) 379-1400

[a] For local sales office, see their catalog.
[b] This company's products are also available through local chemical and laboratory suppliers.
[c] This company's products are available only through local suppliers.

14. *Fluka*, AG
    Buchs, SG, Switzerland
    085-62156

15. *Fox* Chemical Co.
    1556 Industrial Street
    Los Angeles, Calif. 90021
    (213) 627-6059

16. *Hamilton Co.*
    P.O. Box 307
    Whittier, Calif. 90608
    (213) 698-0751

17. *Henley* and Co.
    202 East 44th Street
    New York, N.Y. 10017
    (212) 986-5544

18. *Kontes* Glass Co.
    Vineland, N.J. 08360
    (609) 692-8500

    Kontes of Illinois
    9943 West Franklin Avenue
    Franklin Park, Ill. 60131
    Chicago: (312) 625-4418
    Suburbs: (312) 678-7060

    Kontes of California
    2809 - 10th Street
    Berkeley, Calif. 94710
    (415) 849-2415

    Lab Glass, Inc. (see Cal-Glass)

19. *Laboratory Glass Appar*atus
    1429 Oregon Street
    Berkeley, Calif. 94702
    (415) 849-3430

20. *Mace* Corp.
    1810 Floradale Avenue
    South El Monte, Calif. 91733
    (213) 443-3104

21. *Mallinckrodt* Chemical Works[a,b]
    2nd and Mallinckrodt Streets
    St. Louis, Mo. 63160
    (314) 231-8980

22. *Mann* Research Laboratories
    136 Liberty Street
    New York, N.Y. 10006
    (212) 233-5863

23. The *Matheson* Co., Inc.[a]
    P.O. Box 85
    East Rutherford, N.J. 07073
    (201) 933-2400
    (Direct line from N.Y.C., 947-6397)

24. Matheson, Coleman, *and Bell*[a,b]
    2909 Highland Avenue
    Norwood (Cincinnati), Ohio 45212
    (513) 631-3220

    East Rutherford, N.J. 07073
    (201) 933-2400

    P.O. Box 7203
    Los Angeles, Calif. 90022
    (213) 685-5280

25. *Merck* and Company[b]
    126 East Lincoln Avenue
    Rahway, N.J. 07065
    (201) 381-5000

26. *Microchem*ical Specialties Co.
    1825 Eastshore Highway
    Berkeley, Calif. 94710
    (415) 843-1282

27. *Milton Roy* Co.
    P.O. Box 12169
    St. Petersburg, Fla. 33733
    (813) 544-2581

28. *Nalgene* Plastics[c]
    Nalge Co., Rochester, N.Y.

29. *Nutritional* Biochemicals Corp.
    26201 Miles Road
    Cleveland, Ohio 44128
    (216) 662-0212

30. *Pierce* Chemical Company
    P.O. Box 117
    Rockford, Ill. 61105
    (815) 968-0747

[a] For local sales office, see their catalog.
[b] This company's products are also available through local chemical and laboratory suppliers.
[c] This company's products are available only through local suppliers.

31. *Pyrex* Laboratory Glassware[a,c]
    Corning, N.Y.
    (607) 962-4444

32. *Scientific Glass* Apparatus Company[a]
    Bloomfield, N.J. 07003
    (201) 748-6600
    (Direct line from N.Y.C., 267-9451)

    2375 Pratt Boulevard
    Elk Grove Village, Ill. 60007
    (312) 439-2500

    1801 Via Burton
    Fullerton, Calif. 92632
    (714) 776-2010

33. *Scientific Products*
    1210 Leon Place
    Evanston, Ill. 60201
    (312) 869-0900

    4000 - 170th Street
    Flushing, N.Y. 11358
    (212) 461-5100

    150 Jefferson Drive
    Menlo Park, Calif. 94028
    (415) 323-7741

34. *Schwarz* Bioresearch, Inc.
    Orangeburg, N.Y. 10962
    (914) 359-2700
    (Direct line from N.Y.C., 292-5686)

    Van Nuys, Calif. 91401
    (213) 787-7711

35. *Spinco*/Beckman
    1117 California Avenue
    Palo Alto, Calif. 94304
    (415) 326-1970

36. *Thermovac* Industries
    41 Decker Street
    Copiague, N.Y. 11726
    (516) 691-9050

37. *Toho* Kasei Co., Ltd.
    Kamifukuido 2
    Higashi-Sumiyoshi-Ku
    Osaka, Japan
    (791) 8221

38. B. *Ungerleider* Co.
    92 Centre Street
    Nutley, N.J. 07110
    (201) 661-0995

39. *Van Waters* and Rogers, Inc.[a]
    3745 Bayshore Blvd.
    Brisbane, Calif.
    (415) 467-2600

    P.O. Box 3200, Rincon Annex
    San Francisco, Calif. 94119

40. Paul V. *Yeager*
    Glass Consulting
    414 "J" Street
    Chula Vista, Calif. 92010
    (714) 422-4532

---

[a] For local sales office, see their catalog.

[b] This company's products are also available through local chemical and laboratory suppliers.

[c] This company's products are available only through local suppliers.

Appendix B
GLASSWARE AND APPARATUS

Full names of suppliers are listed in Appendix A. Prices are approximate, and are intended only as a guide. There are other sources for many of the items, and those items listed without a supplier's name are readily available from laboratory supply houses.

Item	Manufacturer, catalog no., approximate price
1. Mechanical shaker for solid phase synthesis, 26-rpm motor, $5\frac{1}{4}''$ between clamp and base. Be sure that the distance between the clamp and base will accommodate your reaction vessel (see Figure 18).	Mann 00701-8138, $123.
2. Reaction vessels (see Figure 24): a. large, 10 g resin b. medium, 5 g resin c. small, 1 g resin (Vessels are made to order, except for Mann, which stocks them.)	Berkeley Glass, $24; Mann 00701-6681, $30. Berkeley Glass, $24. Lab. Glass Appar., $20. Yeager, $25.
3. Cleavage vessels (see Figure 25): a. large b. small (Vessels are made to order.)	Berkeley Glass, $25; Mann 00701-6684, $28. Lab. Glass Appar., $20. Yeager, $25.
4. Adapter, gas inlet, $\mathbf{\$}$ 24/40, inner joint (see Figure 17).	Kontes K 18100, Cal-Glass LG 2050, Sci. Glass JA-7970; $4.
5. Adapter, reducing bushing type $\mathbf{\$}$ 24/40, outer joint, to 14/35, inside (see Figure 22).	Kontes K 15075, size D2; Cal-Glass LG 1240, size C2; Pyrex 8825; Sci. Glass JA-2250; $3.
6. Adapter, rubber, for bleed tubes, fits over $\mathbf{\$}$ 10/18 joints (see Figures 19 and 22).	Kontes K 77390; $2 per doz.
7. Adapter, thermometer, $\mathbf{\$}$ 14/20 inner joint at bottom, serrated hose connection at side, 10/18 joint at top (see Figures 19 and 22).	Kontes K 27625, Cal-Glass ML 287, Sci. Glass JA-7290; $4.
8. Adapter, vacuum, $\mathbf{\$}$ 24/40 outer at top, inner at bottom, serrated hose connection at side.	Kontes K 20500, Cal-Glass LG 1840, Sci. Glass JA-7730; $5.
9. Adapter, vacuum, same as item 8 except $\mathbf{\$}$ 14/20 (see Figures 19 and 22).	Kontes K 27675, Cal-Glass ML 375, Pyrex MW 96860; $5.

10. Adapter, vacuum, ᛋ 24/40, vacuum take-off type, bent 105°.

Kontes K 20550, Cal-Glass LG 1860, Sci. Glass JA-8210; $5.

11. Condenser, air, ᛋ 24/40 inner joint at one end, 550-mm.

Pyrex 91340, Sci. Glass JC-7050; $3.

12. Condenser, water, West, 300-mm, ᛋ at bottom 24/40, top tooled for #3 stopper.

Kontes K 45250, Cal-Glass LG 5330, Sci. Glass JC-8400; $6.

13. Distilling column, Vigreaux ᛋ 24/40, 600-mm, outer joint at top, inner joint at bottom.

Kontes K 50350-2C, Cal-Glass LG 5890, Sci. Glass JD-5060; $14.

14. Distilling head, Claisen, with special ᛋ West-type condenser with bent lower end for direct connection to receiving flask. All ᛋ joints 24/40 except ᛋ 10/30 for thermometer.

Kontes K 51300, Cal-Glass LG 6060; $18.

15. Drying tube, Bantam-ware, U-shaped, with ᛋ 14/20 inner joint, single-bulb desiccant chamber.

Kontes K 29120, Cal-Glass ML 1845, Sci. Glass JM-1450; $3.

16. Drying tube, same as item 15 but with 105° bend.

Kontes K 29110, Cal-Glass ML 1850, Sci. Glass JM-1435; $3.

17. Flasks, round-bottom, short-neck, ᛋ 24/40 outer joint:
    a. 50 ml.
    b. 100 ml.
    c. 5,000 ml.

Kontes K 60100, Pyrex 4320A; $3.
Kontes K 60100, Pyrex 4320; $3.
Kontes K 60100, Pyrex 93240; $6.

18. Funnel, addition, cylindrical, graduated, with pressure-equalizing line and teflon stopcock, ᛋ 24/40 joints, 250 ml (see Figure 17).

Kontes K 63453, Cal-Glass LG 8271T; $26

19. Funnel, powder, Bantam-ware, ᛋ 14/20 inner joint.

Kontes K 29800, Cal-Glass ML 1360, Pyrex MW 94601; $4.

20. Gas-washing bottle, 250 ml, inlet and outlet sealed to ᛋ 24/40 outer stopper (see Figure 22).

Cal-Glass LG 3690, Sci. Glass JB-1370; $7.

21. Two-stage gas regulator with needle valve, for hydrogen cylinder (for hydrogenation at atmospheric pressure).

Matheson Model 8 (CGA 350 connection), $48.

22. Hydrogenator, low-pressure shaker type, Parr Series 3910.

Van Waters 19790, Sci. Glass C-1610; $352.

23. Lecture bottle holders, nontip stand (cadmium-plated steel).

Matheson Model 505; $3.

24. Receiver, distilling, Dean-Stark. — Sci. Glass JD-8020; $15.

25. Rotary evaporator, Buchler, flash-evaporator for batch operation; 2-liter evaporator and condenser flasks with $ 24/40 joints and thermoregulator. — Buchler FE-2 and TR-1, Van Waters 27567 and 27576, Scientific Products E 5250 and E 5210; $216 and $60.

26. Sealing device, aluminum, seal crimper (to seal bottles of pure solvents with rubber stopples for hypodermic needle). — Thermovac SV-SCR, $60.

27. Stopper, medium-length, Penny head, hollow or solid, closed-bottom, $ 14/20. — Kontes K 85050, Cal Glass LG 10310, Pyrex 96508; $2.

28. Stopper, $ 24/40, polyethylene. — Sci. Glass S-8305-3, $0.35.

29. Thin-layer chromatography equipment. — Brinkmann, Sci. Glass.

30. Time switch, Tork no. 919. — Sci. Glass C-6428, $16.

31. Tube, connecting-distilling, $ 24/40 inner joint sealed to 8-mm O.D. side arm at 75° angle (for connecting flasks to vacuum line). — Pyrex 97140, Kontes 17400, Sci. Glass JA-3390; $3.

32. Vacuum line, plastic, for anhydrous HF (see Figure 20). — Toho, $675 (plus shipping and duty, about $250). Ungerleider, $964 total.

33. Valve, Teflon, for HF line. — Mace, $55 (other types also available).

34. Viton O-rings, for HF vessels. — Conover.

35. Bottles, polypropylene screw-cap. — Nalgene.

36. Burette, 25 ml (for chloride analysis).

37. Drying tubes.

38. Fritted glass Buchner funnels, coarse porosity, 20-mm and 30-mm.

39. Heating mantle for 5,000-ml round-bottom flask.

40. Hot plate (for open reflux hydrolysis of peptides).

41. Magnetic stirrer and magnetic stirring bars (for atmospheric hydrogenation, chloride analysis, sodium-NH_3 reduction, etc.).

42. Needle valves for HCl and HBr lecture bottles.   Baker, Matheson.

43. Oil bath with electric immersion heater (for coupling first amino acid to resin).

44. Polyethylene tubing and stopcocks.   Bel-Art.

45. Powerstat, variable transformer for heater.

46. Pumps, metering.   Beckman, Accu-Flow; Milton Roy, Mini-pump.

47. Suction flask, 2,000-ml.

48. Tees, polypropylene.   Bel-Art.

49. Tubes, polypropylene, 18 by 120 mm (for alkaline hydrolysis).   Bel-Art.

50. Thermometer, 250°, $ 10/18.

51. Vacuum gauge for water aspirator.

52. Valve for nitrogen gas.   Baker, Matheson.

53. Varigrad.   Buchler.

54. Vial, Teflon (for alkaline hydrolysis)   Microchem. O-9980, $9.

55. Water aspirator.

Appendix C
CHEMICALS AND REAGENTS

Items listed without a supplier are available widely.

1. The resin, polystyrene-2% divinyl benzene copolymer beads. Bio-Rad (Bio-Beads S-X2), Fluka.
2. Chloromethyl resin. Sold as Merrifield's peptide resin. (Some lots of resin have been reported to give very low conjugation of amino acids to the resin.) Bio-Rad, Cyclo, Mann, Schwarz, $1 per g; in Europe, Fluka (price somewhat lower).
3. Boc amino acids. *All Boc amino acids must be tested for purity by TLC.* Cyclo, Fox, Mann, Schwarz; in Europe, Fluka. Many derivatives are available in addition to those already listed in catalogs. Prices vary from $8 to $35 per g, and vary somewhat among the manufacturers.
4. Boc amino acid-resins. Schwarz and Mann, $25 to $45 for 3 g.
5. Aoc amino acids may be obtained through Dr. S. Sakakibara, Institute for Protein Research, Osaka University, 36 Joancho, Kita-Ku, Osaka, Japan. Prices are significantly lower than for Boc amino acids.
6. Nps amino acids. (Commercial samples may be very impure, the chief contaminant usually being Nps chloride.) Cyclo, Fluka.

7. Acetic acid, glacial (pint bottles are best for avoiding water absorption).
8. Aluminum oxide, for dioxane purification. Use only Merck 71707. Acid-washed alumina is not suitable.
9. Aminopeptidase M. Henley.
10. Ammonia, gas (for Na–NH$_3$ reduction). Baker, Matheson.
11. Ammonium acetate.
12. Ammonium thiocyanate (NH$_4$SCN, for chloride analysis).
13. Anisole, reagent grade (for protection of amino acids during cleavage). Aldrich, Eastman, M C and B.
14. Benzene, anhydrous (keep over KOH).
15. Bromine (for arginine assay).
16. 1-Butanol, reagent grade (n-butanol).
17. t-Butoxycarbonyl azide (for synthesis of Boc amino acids). Aldrich.
18. t-Butyl carbazate (for preparation of t-butoxycarbonyl azide). Aldrich, Cyclo.
19. t-Butyl hypochlorite (for chlorine peptide spray). Nutritional.
20. Carbonyldiimidazole (coupling to hydroxymethyl resin). Aldrich, Fluka.
21. Celite (diatomaceous earth filter aid).
22. Calcium chloride, anhydrous, 8-mesh.
23. Calcium gluconate (for HF decontamination). M C and B.
24. Chloroform, reagent grade.
25. Chloromethyl methyl ether (for chloromethylation of resin). Eastman.
26. Chromatography paper. Whatman no. 1, no. 4, and 3MM.
27. Citric acid, reagent grade (for synthesis of Boc amino acids).
28. Clorox bleach (sodium hypochlorite solution, 5.25%, for peptide spray).

29. Cobalt trifluoride (for drying HF). M C and B.
30. Cupric sulfate pentahydrate (for Folin-Lowry assay).
31. Dicyclohexylcarbodiimide (DCC). Aldrich, Schwarz, Fluka.
32. Dimethylformamide (DMF). All grades from any supplier must be purified.
33. Dimethyl sulfoxide (for synthesis of Boc amino acids). Eastman, M C and B.
34. Dioxane, peroxide-free.
35. Drierite, indicating, 8-mesh (anhydrous $CaSO_4$).
36. Ethanol, absolute (for washing peptide-resin), 95% (for peptide spray).
37. Ether, USP (for extraction).
38. Ethyl acetate (for extraction).
39. Ethyl methyl sulfide (for protection of certain amino acids during cleavage). Eastman.
40. Ferric alum ($FeNH_4 (SO_4)_2 \cdot 12H_2O$, for chloride analysis).
41. Fluorodinitrobenzene (FDNB, for assay of DMF purity). Eastman, M C and B.
42. Folin-Ciocalteau phenol reagent (for Folin-Lowry assay). Fisher.
43. Glass wool.
44. Hexane (petroleum ether, b.p. 60–70°).
45. Hydrazine hydrate. Eastman, M C and B.
46. Hydrogen (H_2). Baker, Matheson.
47. Hydrindantin. Pierce.
48. Hydrochloric acid, concentrated, highest purity (avoid NH_3 absorption).
49. Hydrogen bromide gas, anhydrous, lecture-bottle size. Ask for extra lead washers. Baker, Matheson.
50. Hydrogen chloride gas, anhydrous, lecture-bottle size. Baker, Matheson.
51. Hydrogen fluoride gas, anhydrous. Baker, Matheson.
52. Magnesium oxide, reagent grade (for synthesis of Boc amino acids).
53. Magnesium sulfate, anhydrous, reagent grade.
54. 2-Mercaptoethanol. Eastman.
55. Methanol, reagent grade.
56. Methyl cellosolve (methoxy ethanol, for quantitative ninhydrin assay and synthesis of hydroxymethyl resin). Aldrich, Eastman, M C and B.
57. Methylene chloride (CH_2Cl_2, dichloromethane), reagent grade.
58. 1-Naphthol (for arginine assay). Aldrich, Eastman.
59. Ninhydrin. Pierce.
60. Nitric acid, 70% (for chloride and tyrosine assay).
61. Nitric acid, fuming, 90% (for nitro resin synthesis).
62. γ-p-Nitrobenzyl glutamate. Cyclo.
63. p-Nitrophenol (synthesis of active esters). Aldrich, Eastman, M C and B.
64. 1-Nitroso-2-naphthol (for tyrosine spray). Aldrich, Eastman, M C and B.
65. Papain. Mann.
66. Potassium hydroxide, reagent grade (for drying).
67. Potassium iodide (for peroxide test and chlorine peptide spray).
68. 5% Pd on $BaSO_4$. M C and B Engelhard.
69. Potassium acetate, anhydrous, reagent grade.
70. Pyridine.
71. Resin: Dowex 1 × 2; Bio-Rad AG 1 × 2, 200–400 mesh.
    Dowex 50; Bio-Rad AG 50W-X2.
    IRC-50; Rohm and Haas XE-64, Mallinckrodt CG-50, 200-400 mesh.

72. Resorcinol, reagent grade (for protection of certain amino acids during cleavage). Aldrich, Eastman, M C and B.
73. Silica gels. Merck G or H (for TLC). Brinkmann.
74. Silver nitrate (for chloride assay).
75. Sodium, metal (for reductive deprotection).
76. Sodium chloride (for chloride assay).
77. Sodium potassium tartrate (for Folin-Lowry assay).
78. Stannic chloride (for chloromethylation). M C and B.
79. TLC plates: silica-gel coated glass; Brinkman.
    silica-gel coated plastic; Eastman (chromagram sheets, type K 301 R2, without fluorescent indicator), Brinkmann (MN Polygram Sil S-HR).
    glass or plastic, coated with cellulose powder; Brinkmann MN Polygram 300 cell.
80. Thioacetamide (for removal of Nps groups). Eastman, Fisher, M C and B.
81. o-Tolidine (for chlorine peptide spray). Eastman.
82. Toluene (for chloride assay).
83. Triethyl amine. Eastman white label or equivalent; redistill if it has any color.
84. Trimethyl amine acetate. Eastman, Fisher, M C and B.
85. Trifluoroacetic acid. Eastman, Pierce; use only if it is colorless.
86. Urea (for arginine assay).

Appendix D
MOLECULAR WEIGHTS OF AMINO ACIDS AND DERIVATIVES

Amino Acid	Abbreviation	Amino acid molecular weight	Boc amino acid molecular weight[a]
Alanine	Ala	89.1	189.1
Arginine	Arg	174.2	NO$_2$-319.2, Tos-353.1
Aspartic acid	Asp	133.1	β-OBzl-323.1
Asparagine	Asn	132.1	232.1, ONp-353.1
Cysteine	Cys	121.2	S-Bzl-311.2, S-MeOBzl-341.2
Cystine	(Cys)$_2$	240.3	440.3
Diidotyrosine	Tyr(I$_2$)	433.0	533.0
Glutamic acid	Glu	147.1	γ-OBzl-337.1, γ-OBzlNO$_2$-382.1
Glutamine	Gln	146.0	246.0, ONp-367.0
Glycine	Gly	75.1	175.0
Histidine	His	155.2	im-Bzl-345.2, im-Dnp-308.0
Hydroxyproline	Hyp	131.1	231.1
Isoleucine	Ile	131.2	231.2
Leucine	Leu	131.2	231.2
Lysine	Lys	146.2	Z-380.0, For-274.2
Methionine	Met	149.2	249.2
Norleucine	Nle	131.2	231.2
Ornithine	Orn	133.0	Z-367.0
Phenylalanine	Phe	165.2	265.2
Proline	Pro	115.1	215.1
Serine	Ser	105.1	O-Bzl-295.1
Threonine	Thr	119.1	219.1, OBzl-309.1
Tryptophan	Trp	204.2	304.2
Tyrosine	Tyr	181.2	OBzl-371.2, MeOBzl-401.2
Valine	Val	117.1	217.1

[a] Other protecting groups (see Appendix E) attached to the Boc amino acid are given before the molecular weight.

Appendix E
PROTECTING GROUPS AND REAGENTS

Acetyl	$CH_3-\overset{\overset{\displaystyle O}{\|}}{C}-$	Ac	42
tert-Amyloxycarbonyl	$CH_3CH_2-\overset{\overset{\displaystyle CH_3}{\|}}{\underset{\underset{\displaystyle CH_3}{\|}}{C}}-O-\overset{\overset{\displaystyle O}{\|}}{C}-$	Aoc	114
Benzoyl	$C_6H_5-\overset{\overset{\displaystyle O}{\|}}{C}-$	Bz	104
Benzyl	$C_6H_5-CH_2-$	Bzl	90
Benzyloxycarbonyl (carbobenzoxy)	$C_6H_5-CH_2-O-\overset{\overset{\displaystyle O}{\|}}{C}-$	Z	135
tert-Butyloxycarbonyl	$CH_3-\overset{\overset{\displaystyle CH_3}{\|}}{\underset{\underset{\displaystyle CH_3}{\|}}{C}}-O-\overset{\overset{\displaystyle O}{\|}}{C}-$	Boc	100
1-Carbobenzoxamido, 2,2,2-trifluoroethyl (Weygand for *im*-His)	$C_6H_5-CH_2-O-\overset{\overset{\displaystyle O}{\|}}{C}-NH-\overset{\overset{\displaystyle CF_3}{\|}}{\underset{\underset{\displaystyle H}{\|}}{C}}-$	Ztf	217
2,4-Dinitrophenyl (*im*-His)	$O_2N-C_6H_3-NO_2$	Dnp	153
Formyl	$H-\overset{\overset{\displaystyle O}{\|}}{C}-$	For	28
p-Methoxybenzyl (Cys and Tyr)	$CH_3-O-C_6H_4-CH_2-$	MeOBzl	120

Name	Formula	Abbreviation	Weight to be added to molecular weight
o-Nitrophenylsulfenyl	(o-nitrophenyl)—S— structure with —NO$_2$	Nps	153 (free acid)
p-Toluenesulfonyl	CH$_3$—(phenyl)—SO$_2$—	Tos	154

Carboxyl protecting and activating groups

Name	Formula	Abbreviation	Weight to be added to molecular weight
Benzyl ester	(phenyl)—CH$_2$—	OBzl	90
N-hydroxysuccinimide ester	succinimide structure with two O and N—	OSu	133
p-Nitrobenzyl ester	O$_2$N—(phenyl)—CH$_2$—	O—BzlNO$_2$	135
p-Nitrophenyl ester	O$_2$N—(phenyl)—	ONp	121
Phenyl ester	(phenyl)—	OPh	76

Other chemicals

Name	Formula	Abbreviation	Molecular weight
Anisole (d 1.0)	CH$_3$O—(phenyl)		108
Carbonyldiimidazole	N N—C(=O)—N N (two imidazole rings)		162
Dicyclohexylamine (d 0.925)	(cyclohexyl)—NH—(cyclohexyl)	DCHA	181
Dicyclohexylcarbodiimide	(cyclohexyl)—N=C=N—(cyclohexyl)	DCC	206
Ethyl methyl sulfide (d 0.837)	C$_2$H$_5$—S—CH$_3$		78

Name	Formula	Abbreviation	Weight to be added to molecular weight
N-ethyl-5-phenylisoxazolium-3'-sulfonate (Woodward's reagent)			253
Resorcinol			110
Triethyl amine (d 0.723)	$(C_2H_5)_3N$	Et_3N	101
t-Butyloxycarbonyl azide (d 1.01)	$(CH_3)_3C-O-\overset{\overset{\displaystyle O}{\|}}{C}N_3$		143

Appendix F
REPRESENTATIVE PEPTIDES PREPARED BY SPPS

Number of Amino Acid Residues	Peptide	Reference
(2-6)	(Several small peptides)	–
6	Secretin hexapeptide amide	15
7	Eledoisin analog	120
8	Angiotensin II and analogs	47, 65, 95
9	Bradykinin	72
8, 9, 10	Approximately 100 bradykinin analogs	127, 128, 132
9	Vasopressin	70
9	Oxytocin and analogs	5, 44, 59, 135
10	Tobacco mosaic virus peptide	133, 143
11	Methionyl-lysyl-bradykinin	74
11	Immunogenic DNP peptide	100
12	Dodeca-proline	134
15	Cytochrome C peptide	52
17	Angiotensinyl-bradykinin	75
18	Bradykininyl-bradykinin	88
18	Polistes kinin	127
21	Bovine insulin A-chain and analogs	61, 62, 139
30	Bovine insulin B-chain	62
55	Clostridium ferredoxin	6

REFERENCES

1. G. W. Anderson and A. C. McGregor, *J. Am. Chem. Soc.* **79**, 6180 (1957).
2. J. L. Bailey, *Techniques in Protein Chemistry* (Elsevier, 1967).
3. J. L. Bailey and R. D. Cole, *J. Biol. Chem.* **234**, 1733 (1959).
4. A Battersby and J. C. Robinson, *J. Chem. Soc.* (1955), p. 259.
5. E. Bayer and H. Hagenmaier, *Tetrahedron Letters*, no. 17 (March 1968), p. 2037.
6. E. Bayer, G. Jung, and H. Hagenmaier, *Tetrahedron* **24**, 4853 (1968).
7. Beckman Instruments, Spinco Division, Palo Alto, Calif.
8. W. F. Benisek and R. D. Cole, *Biochem. Biophys. Res. Commun.* **20**, 655 (1965); *Biochemistry* **6**, 3780 (1967).
9. A. Berger, personal communication to R. B. Merrifield. See also A. Yaron and S. F. Schlossman, *Biochemistry* **7**, 267 (1968).
10. H. C. Beyerman, C. A. M. Boers-Boonekamp, and H. Massen van den Brink-Zimmermanova, *Rec. Trav. Chim.* **87**, 1 (1968).
11. H. C. Beyerman, C. A. M. Boers-Boonekamp, W. J. van Zoest, and D. van den Berg, in (12), p. 117.
12. H. C. Beyerman, A. van de Linde, and W. M. van den Brink, eds., *Peptides* (Wiley, 1967).
13. M. Bodanszky and M. A. Ondetti, *Peptide Synthesis* (Interscience, 1966).
14. M. Bodanszky and J. T. Sheehan, *Chem. Ind. London* (1964), p. 1423.
15. M. Bodanszky and J. T. Sheehan, *Chem. Ind. London* (1966), p. 1597.
16. M. Bodanszky and V. du Vigneaud, *J. Am. Chem. Soc.* **81**, 5688 (1959).
17. F. M. Bumpus, M. C. Khosla, and R. R. Smeby, Abstract M 40, 153rd Annual Meeting, *Am. Chem. Soc.*, April 1967.
18. L. A. Carpino, *J. Am. Chem. Soc.* **82**, 2725 (1960).
19. L. A. Carpino, C. A. Giza, and B. A. Carpino, *J. Am. Chem. Soc.* **81**, 955 (1959).
20. L. C. Craig, P. Alexander, and R. J. Block, eds., *Analytical Methods of Protein Chemistry* (Pergamon, 1960), I, 121.
21. L. C. Craig and D. Craig, in A. Weissburger, ed., *Technique of Organic Chemistry*, vol. III, part 1 (Interscience, 2nd ed., 1956), p. 149.
22. L. C. Dorman and J. Love, Abstract P 146, 155th Annual Meeting, *Am. Chem. Soc.*, April 1968.
23. Y. C. Du, R. Q. Jiang, and C. L. Tsou, *Sci. Sinica* **14**, 230 (1965).
24. C. W. Easley, *Biochim. Biophys. Acta* **107**, 386 (1965).
25. A. B. Edmundson, in (36), p. 369.
26. A. Felix, personal communication.
27. M. Fridkin, A. Patchornik, and E. Katchalski, *J. Am. Chem. Soc.* **87**, 4646 (1965).
28. G. Funatsu, *Biochemistry* **3**, 1351 (1964).
29. O. Grahl-Nielsen and G. Tritsch, Abstract C 266, 154th Annual Meeting, *Am. Chem. Soc.*, Sept. 1967.
30. O. Grahl-Nielsen and G. Tritsch, personal communication.
31. J. B. Greenstein and M. Winitz, *Chemistry of the Amino Acids* (Wiley, 1961), vol. II.
32. S. Guttmann and R. A. Boissonnas, *Helv. Chim. Acta* **42**, 1257 (1959).
33. P. B. Hawk, B. L. Oser, and W. H. Summerson, *Practical Physiological Chemistry* (Blakiston, 13th ed., 1954), p. 955.
34. R. J. Hill, in (36), pp. 173, 378.
35. C. H. W. Hirs, in (36), p. 328.
36. C. H. W. Hirs, ed., *Methods in Enzymology* (Academic Press, 1967), vol. XI.
37. I. Honda, Y. Shimonishi, and S. Sakakibara, *Bull. Chem. Soc. Japan* **40**, 2415 (1967).
38. D. B. Hope, V. Murti, and V. du Vigneaud, *J. Biol. Chem.* **237**, 1563 (1962).
39. S. Hörnle, *Z. Physiol. Chem.* **348**, 1355 (1967).
40. N. Inukai, K. Nakano, and M. Murakami, *Bull. Chem. Soc. Japan* **41**, 182 (1968).
41. F. Irrevere, *Biochim. Biophys. Acta* **111**, 551 (1965).
42. B. M. Iselin, *Helv. Chim. Acta* **44**, 61 (1961).
43. B. M. Iselin, in L. Zervas, ed., *Peptides* (Pergamon, 1965), p. 27.
44. D. A. J. Ives, personal communication.
45. W. Kessler and B. M. Iselin, *Helv. Chim. Acta* **49**, 1330 (1966).
46. H. T. Keutmann and J. T. Potts, personal communication.
47. M. C. Khosla, R. R. Smeby, and F. M. Bumpus,

Biochemistry **6**, 754 (1967).

48. M. C. Khosla, R. R. Smeby, and F. M. Bumpus, *Science* **156**, 253 (1967).
49. J. G. Kirchner, *Thin Layer Chromatography* (Interscience, 1967).
50. K. D. Kopple, R. R. Jarabak, and P. L. Bhatia, *Biochemistry* **2**, 958 (1963).
51. R. Khun and H. J. Haas, *Angew. Chem.* **67**, 785 (1955).
52. J. Lenard and A. B. Robinson, *J. Am. Chem. Soc.* **89**, 181 (1967).
53. J. Lenard, A. V. Schally, and G. P. Hess, *Biochem. Biophys. Res. Commun.* **14**, 498 (1964).
54. R. L. Letsinger, M. J. Kornet, V. Mahadevan, and D. M. Jerina, *J. Am. Chem. Soc.* **86**, 5163 (1964).
55. A. Loffet, *Experientia* **23**, 406 (1967).
56. M. E. Lombardo and R. Piasio, personal communication.
57. M. E. Lombardo, R. Piasio, and J. M. Stewart, unpublished.
58. D. H. Lowry, N. H. Rosebrough, and A. L. Farr, *J. Biol. Chem.* **193**, 265 (1951).
59. J. M. P. Manning, *J. Am. Chem. Soc.* **90**, 1348 (1968).
60. A. Marglin and T. Tanimura, personal communication.
61. A. Marglin and S. Cushman, *Biochem. Biophys. Res. Commun.* **29**, 710 (1967).
62. A. Marglin and R. B. Merrifield, *J. Am. Chem. Soc.* **88**, 5051 (1966).
63. G. R. Marshall, personal communication.
64. G. R. Marshall, in N. Back, R. Paoletti, and L. Martini, eds., *Milan Symposium on Peptides and Proteins* (Plenum, 1968).
65. G. R. Marshall and R. B. Merrifield, *Biochemistry* **4**, 2394 (1965).
66. G. R. Marshall, R. B. Merrifield, and J. M. Stewart, unpublished.
67. R. H. Mazur, B. W. Ellis, and F. S. Cammarata, *J. Biol. Chem.* **237**, 1619 (1962).
68. M. A. McDowell and E. L. Smith, *J. Biol. Chem.* **240**, 4635 (1965).
69. H. Medzhihradsky-Schweiger and K. Medzhihradsky, *Acta Chim. Acad. Sci. Hung.* **50**, 339 (1966).
70. J. Meienhofer and Y. Sano, *J. Am. Chem. Soc.* **90**, 2996 (1968).
71. R. B. Merrifield, *J. Am. Chem. Soc.* **85**, 2149 (1963).
72. R. B. Merrifield, *J. Am. Chem. Soc.* **86**, 304 (1964).
73. R. B. Merrifield, *Biochemistry* **3**, 1385 (1964).
74. R. B. Merrifield, *J. Org. Chem.* **29**, 3100 (1964).
75. R. B. Merrifield, *Recent Progress Hormone Res.* **23**, 451 (1967).
76. R. B. Merrifield, in H. A. Sober, ed., *Handbook of Biochemistry* (Chemical Rubber, 1968).
77. R. B. Merrifield, unpublished.
78. R. B. Merrifield and M. A. Corigliano, unpublished.
79. R. B. Merrifield and M. A. Corigliano, *Biochem. Preparation* **12**, 98 (1968).
80. R. B. Merrifield and A. Marglin, in (12), p. 85.
81. R. B. Merrifield, J. M. Stewart, and N. Jernberg, *Anal. Chem.* **38**, 1905 (1966).
82. R. B. Merrifield and J. M. Stewart, *Nature* **207**, 522 (1965).
83. T. Mizoguchi, unpublished.
84. T. Mizoguchi, G. Levin, D. W. Woolley, and J. M. Stewart, *J. Org. Chem.* **33**, 903 (1968).
85. T. Mizoguchi and D. W. Woolley, *J. Med. Chem.* **10**, 251 (1967).
86. S. Moore, personal communication.
87. S. Moore and W. H. Stein, *J. Biol. Chem.* **211**, 907 (1954).
88. V. A. Najjar and R. B. Merrifield, *Biochemistry* **5**, 3765 (1966).
89. H. Nesvadba and H. Roth, *Monatsch. Chem.* **98**, 1432 (1967).
90. N. P. Neumann, in (36), p. 487.
91. D. E. Nitecki, personal communication.
92. D. E. Nitecki and J. W. Goodman, *Biochemistry* **5**, 665 (1966).
93. M. Ohno and C. B. Anfinsen, *J. Am. Chem. Soc.* **89**, 5994 (1967).
94. D. Ontjes and A. Marglin, personal communication.
95. W. K. Park, R. R. Smeby, and F. M. Bumpus, *Biochemistry* **6**, 3458 (1967).
96. G. Pataki, *Techniques of Thin-Layer Chromatography in Amino Acid and Peptide Chemistry* (Ann Arbor Science, 1968).
97. L. M. Pourchot and J. H. Johnson, *Nature* (in press).
98. J. Ramachandran, *Nature* **206**, 927 (1965).
99. W. J. Ray and D. E. Koshland, *J. Biol. Chem.* **237**, 2493 (1962).
100. F. F. Richards, R. W. Sloane, Jr., and E. Haber, *Biochemistry* **6**, 476 (1967).
101. A. B. Robinson, Thesis, University of California at San Diego, 1967.
102. M. Rothe and W. Dunkel, *Polymer Letters* **5**, 589 (1967).

103. S. Sakakibara, personal communication.

104. S. Sakakibara and Y. Shimonishi, *Bull. Chem. Soc. Japan* **38**, 1412 (1965).

105. S. Sakakibara, Y. Shimonishi, Y. Kishida, M. Okada, and H. Sugihara, *Bull. Chem. Soc. Japan* **40**, 2164 (1967).

106. S. Sakakibara, Y. Shimonishi, M. Okada, and Y. Kishida, in (12), p. 44.

107. S. Sakakibara, M. Shin, M. Fujino, Y. Shimonishi, S. Inouye, and N. Inukai, *Bull. Chem. Soc. Japan* **38**, 1522 (1965).

108. S. Sakakibara, K. H. Shin, and G. P. Hess, *J. Am. Chem. Soc.* **84**, 4921 (1962).

109. F. Sanger and E. O. P. Thompson, *Biochim. Biophys. Acta* **71**, 468 (1963).

110. E. Schnabel, *Ann. Chem.* **702**, 188 (1967).

111. J. Schreiber, in (12), p. 107.

112. W. A. Schroeder, in (36), p. 351.

113. E. Schröder and K. Lübke, *The Peptides* (Academic Press, 1965, 1966), 2 vols.

114. E. Schröder and K. Lübke, in (113), I, 175.

115. Schwarz Bioresearch, Orangeburg, N. Y.

116. R. Schwyzer, P. Sieber, and H. Kappeler, *Helv. Chim. Acta* **42**, 2622 (1959).

117. E. P. Semkin, N. D. Gafurova, and L. A. Shchukina, *Khim. Prirodn. Soedin. Akad. Nauk Uz. SSR* **3**, 220 (1967).

118. E. P. Semkin, A. P. Smirnova, and L. A. Shchukina, *Zh. Obshch. Khim.* **37**, 1169 (1967).

119. S. Shaltiel, *Biochem. Biophys. Res. Commun.* **29**, 178 (1967).

120. L. A. Shchukina and L. Yu Sklyarov, *Khim. Prirodn. Soedin. Akad. Nauk Uz. SSR* **2**, 200 (1966); *see Chem. Abstr.* **65**, 17042 (1966).

121. M. Shimizu, personal communication.

122. F. Sipos and G. S. Denning, personal communication.

123. I. Smith, ed., *Chromatographic Techniques* (Interscience, 1960).

124. E. Sondheimer and R. W. Holley, *J. Am. Chem. Soc.* **76**, 2467 (1954).

125. T. F. Spande and B. Witkop, in (36), p. 498.

126. E. Stahl, *Thin-Layer Chromatography* (Springer, 1965).

127. J. M. Stewart, *Federation Proc.* **27**, 63 (1968).

128. J. M. Stewart, unpublished.

129. J. M. Stewart and R. B. Merrifield, unpublished.

130. J. M. Stewart, T. Mizoguchi, and D. W. Woolley, Abstract 0 206, 153rd Annual Meeting, *Am. Chem. Soc.*, April 1967.

131. J. M. Stewart, T. Mizoguchi, and D. W. Woolley, *J. Med. Chem.* (in press).

132. J. M. Stewart and D. W. Woolley, in E. G. Erdos, N. Back, and F. Sicuteri, eds., *Hypotensive Peptides* (Springer, 1966), p. 23.

133. J. M. Stewart, J. D. Young, E. Benjamini, M. Shimizu, and C. Y. Leung, *Biochemistry* **5**, 3396 (1966).

134. L. Stryer and R. P. Haugland, *Proc. Nat. Acad. Sci. U.S.* **58**, 719 (1967).

135. H. Takashima, R. B. Merrifield, and V. du Vigneaud, *J. Am. Chem. Soc.* **90**, 1323 (1968).

136. A. B. Thomas and E. G. Rochow, *J. Am. Chem. Soc.* **79**, 1843 (1957).

137. G. L. Tritsch, personal communication.

138. C. J. Weber, *J. Biol. Chem.* **86**, 217 (1930).

139. U. Weber, S. Hörnle, G. Grieser, K. Herzog, and G. Weitzel, *Z. Physiol. Chem.* **348**, 1715 (1967).

140. F. Weygand and U. Ragnarsson, *Z. Naturforsch.* **21b**, 1141 (1966).

141. F. Weygand, W. Steglich, and P. Pietta, *Chem. Ber.* **100**, 3841 (1967).

142. D. W. Woolley, unpublished.

143. J. D. Young, E. Benjamini, J. M. Stewart, and C. Y. Leung, *Biochemistry* **6**, 1455 (1967).

144. J. D. Young, C. Y. Leung, and W. A. Rombauts, *Biochemistry* **7**, 2475 (1968).

145. H. Zahn, in (12), p. 43.

146. G. Zweig and J. R. Whitaker, *Paper Chromatography and Electrophoresis* (Academic Press, 1967), vol. I.

AUTHOR INDEX

SUBJECT INDEX

A

Abbreviations, xiv, 82–85.

Acetic acid, 6, 18, 30, 34. *See also* Hydrogen chloride in acetic acid.

Acetic anhydride, 9, 32, 33. *See also* Acetylation.

Acetyl group, 83.

Acetylation: during coupling step, 18, 34;
  of *t*-butyloxycarbonyl-*im*-benzyl-histidyl-hydroxy-methyl resin, 33;
  of peptides on resin, 33;
  side reaction on hydroxyl groups, 13, 14.

Acid-labile groups: use of 2-(*p*-biphenylyl)-2-propyl-oxy-carbonyl group, 16–17;
  use of *o*-nitrophenylsulfenyl group, 16.
  See also Tryptophan.

Activated amino acid, 19. *See also* Coupling reactions.

Activation. *See* Coupling reactions; Resin.

Active ester polymers, 5.

Active ester coupling. *See* Coupling reactions; *p*-Nitrophenyl esters.

Acylation. *See* Acetylation.

Acyl urea, 4, 7, 24, 39.

Alanine and derivatives, 60, 82.

Alcohols, transesterification of peptides from resin, 12, 45.

Alcoholysis of amides, 32.

Alumina, for dioxane purification, 18, 31.

Aluminum oxide. *See* Alumina.

ω-Amide functions in coupling, 24. *See also* Glutamine; Asparagine.

Amide synthesis, 12, 13, 44.

Amino acids, 82;
  analysis, 7, 53–55,
    analyzer constants, 53, 54,
    analyzer emergence time, 54;
  derivatives, 82,
    as acyl urea derivatives in resin, 7,
    recovery after SPPS, 25,
    steric hindrance during coupling, 24, 39,
    TLC, 58–61;
  α-amino groups, protection and deprotection, 2–4, 13–19 (*see also* Protecting groups),
  and ε-amino protecting group of lysine, 19–20,
  and histidine protecting group, 20.
  See also specific amino acids.

Amino acid resin preparation. *See* Resin, aminoacyl.

ε-Aminocaproic acid tetramers, 4.

α-Amino groups. *See under* Amino acids; Protection and deprotection of functional groups.

Aminopeptidase M, 54–55.

Ammonia interference, 57, 58.

Ammonia cleavage. *See* Cleavage of peptide resins by ammonolysis.

Ammonium chloride, 42.

Ammonolysis, 12, 13. *See also* Cleavage of peptide resins by ammonolysis.

t-Amyloxyamino acids, 15, 79.

t-Amyloxycarbonyl chloride, 15.

t-Amyloxycarbonyl group, 15–16, 83.

Angiotensin, 11, 50, 86.

Angiotensinyl-bradykinin, 18, 86.

Anion-exchange resin. *See* Cleavage of peptide-resins by transesterification; Column chromatography.

Anisole, 9, 10, 11, 21, 44;
  in HBr-TFA cleavage, 40;
  in HF cleavage, 11, 43–44;
  removal, 41, 44.

Apparatus, 75–78;
  suppliers of, 72–74.

Arginine, 82;
  arginine-proline bonds, 48, 49;
  t-butyloxycarbonyl-toluenesulfonyl arginine, 34;
  nitroarginine, 8, 9,
    analysis of reduced, 46,
    t-butyloxycarbonyl, 34, 60, 82,
    determination of, from peptide hydrolysate, 53,
    emergence time from analyzer, 54,
    enzymatic analysis of, 55,
    reduction, 19, 45, 46,
    UV analysis of, 46;
  peptides, cleavage by sodium in liquid ammonia, 19;
  protecting groups for guanidino function, 19,
    toluenesulfonyl group, 9, 19, 46, 84,
    use without, 19,
  Sakaguchi determination of, 56, 63.

Asparagine, 23, 82;
  active ester for stepwise synthesis on resin, 35;
  analysis by enzymatic hydrolysis, 55;
  derivatives, 30, 82,
    attachment to resin, 32,
    t-butyloxycarboxyl-α-*p*-nitrophenyl ester, 30, 35,
    in stepwise synthesis on resin, 35,

molar amounts in SPPS, 24, 39, 40;
solubility, in dichloromethane, 28,
 in dimethylsulfoxide, 15;
suppliers, 79;
synthesis, 15, 28–30,
 in dimethyl sulfoxide, 29,
 Schnabel method, 15, 28,
 Schwyzer method with magnesium oxide, 29;
TLC Rf's, 60,
 of p-nitrophenyl esters, 61.
 See also specific amino acids.
t-Butyloxycarbonyl aminoacyl resins, 79. *See also* Resin, aminoacyl, *and specific amino acids.*
t-Butyloxycarbonyl azide, 15, 28;
manufacturer, 29, 79;
precautions in use, 29.
t-Butyloxycarbonyl group, 2, 4, 13, 83;
on ε-amino group of lysine, 17;
removal, and ε-benzyloxycarbonyl lysine amino group, 20,
 and hydroxyamino acids, 14,
 and tryptophan lability, 48,
 during hydrazinolysis, 45,
 on TLC plates, 62,
 with HBr-TFA, 9,
 with HCl-HOAc, 14,
 with trifluoroacetic acid, 15, 18, 23.

C

Calcium gluconate, 41.
1-Carbobenzoxamido-2,2,2-trifluoroethyl group, 11, 20, 83.
Carbobenzoxy chloride, 15.
Carbobenzoxy group. *See* Benzyloxycarbonyl group.
Carbon dioxide, 38, 46.
N,N'-Carbonyldiimidazole, 9, 84;
for aminoacyl-hydroxymethyl resin preparation, 33;
for methionyl-hydroxymethyl resin, 9.
ω-Carboxyl function: and side reaction with hydroxyl groups, 22–23;
protecting groups, 20,
 and benzyloxycarbonyl deprotection, 14,
 in transesterification cleavage, 12;
resistance to ammonolysis, 12.
 See also Aspartic acid; Glutamic acid.
Catalysts: for active ester coupling, 26;
poisoning by sulfur amino acids, 19.
 See also Hydrogenolysis.
CBZ group. *See* Benzyloxycarbonyl group.
CCD. *See* Countercurrent distribution.

Cellulose-powder-coated TLC sheets, 60.
Chain branching. *See* Branching.
Chain length. *See* Peptides, length.
Chain termination, 18.
Chemicals: suppliers, 72–74;
 list, 79–81.
Chipco shaker, 68. *See also* Peptide shaker.
Chloride analysis, 6, 55–56.
Chlorine peptide spray, 59, 62.
Chloroform, 6.
Chloromethyl methyl ether, 6, 27.
Chromatographic sprays, 62–64.
Chromatography: column, 50–52;
gas-liquid, 12;
gel, 50, 51;
ion-exchange, 50–52;
paper, 52, 58–61,
 preparative, 52,
 solvents, 52–59;
thin layer, 58–61,
 diastereoisomer separation, 60,
 Rf's, 60, 61,
 solvents, 59–61.
Cleavage of peptide-resins, 3, 4, 9–13, 40–45;
amino acids during,
 arginine, 19,
 benzylation, 21,
 glutamic and aspartic acid protecting groups, 20,
 histidine, protected with Weygand's group, 20,
 serine and threonine, 14,
 tryptophan, 48, 49;
by ammonolysis, 5, 12, 44,
 and tryptophan, 49,
 in synthesis of desamino oxytocin, 12,
 solvents, 12,
 with nitro resins, 12;
by anhydrous HF, 10, 11, 12, 15, 41–44,
 color formation, 43,
 desalting, 44,
 effect on amino acids, 44,
 arginine, 19,
 cysteine protecting groups, 21,
 histidine, 44,
 lysine, ε-benzyloxycarbonyl, 20,
 tryptophan, 10, 49,
 tyrosine, O-benzyl, 23, 44,
 metals, 44,
 N-O acyl migration during, 11, 25, 44,
 N-S acyl migration during, 21,
 precautions, 41–42,
 removal of protecting groups of amino acids, 11, 20,
 scavengers, 21, 43;